THE CHALLENGE OF BERNADETTE

THE CHALLENGE OF BERNADETTE

by
HUGH ROSS WILLIAMSON

LONDON
BURNS & OATES

NIHIL OBSTAT : DANIEL DVIVESTEIJN, S.T.D.

CENSOR DEPVTATVS

IMPRIMATVR : E. MORROGH BERNARD

VICARIVS GENERALIS

WESTMONASTERII : DIE XXIII DECEMBRIS MCMLVII

Copyright © by Burns & Oates 1958

Made and printed in Great Britain
at the Burleigh Press, Lewins Mead, Bristol
for Burns Oates and Washbourne Ltd.
28 Ashley Place, London, S.W.1

TO

MARGARET MILLS

CONTENTS

Preface

THIS is not a biography of St Bernadette. There are now so many biographies of her that it is improbable that any reader will be unacquainted with her story. Yet, lest there should be such a one, it is worth giving, by way of preface, a simple outline of the circumstances which followed the appearance of the Blessed Virgin in a grotto at Massabielle, near Lourdes, a little French township at the foot of the Pyrenees, a hundred years ago.

In 1858 Our Lady appeared to Bernadette, a girl of 14, the eldest of the four children of François Soubirous, a miller who had fallen on evil days. The first apparition was on Thursday, February 11: the last and eighteenth, on Friday, July 16.

On July 28, 1858, an episcopal decree set up a Commission "appointed to decide upon the authenticity and character of the events that have occurred during the last six months, on the occasion of a real or alleged appearance of the Most Blessed Virgin in a grotto situated to the west of the town of Lourdes".

The enquiry continued for two years, during which Bernadette herself was cross-examined in exhaustive detail and every available witness interviewed.

On Saturday, January 18, 1862, the Bishop of Tarbes, in whose diocese Lourdes lies, signed the Pastoral Letter which began: "We judge that the Immaculate Mary, Mother of God, did in actual fact appear to Bernadette Soubirous on 11 February 1858 and on the days following, to the number of eighteen times . . .".

Bernadette saw her standing in a niche, a lancet-pointed

cleft, high up in the rock of Massabielle. She appeared as a
girl, scarcely older than Bernadette herself, not very tall and
of indescribable beauty. She was dressed in a white gown,
bound in at the waist with a blue sash. Over her head was
a white veil. Her feet were bare but covered by the lowest
folds of the gown, except at the point where a yellow rose
shone upon each of them. On her right arm was a rosary of
white beads on a gold chain.

In her various appearances she spoke to the child in the
Lourdes *patois*.

"Will you kindly come here for a fortnight? . . . I do not
promise to make you happy in this world but in the world
to come . . . Pray to God for sinners . . . Penance, penance,
penance . . . Go and tell the priests to build a chapel here . . .
I want people to come here in procession . . . Go and drink
of the spring and wash in it: go and eat of the grass you
find there . . . I am the Immaculate Conception; I wish for
a chapel here."

In addition to these sayings, she revealed to Bernadette a
special form of prayer and three personal secrets which
were never divulged.

No one but Bernadette saw Our Lady, though on the last
day of the "fortnight", Thursday, March 4, the police
estimate of the crowd at the Grotto was twenty thousand.

The spring which Our Lady pointed out to Bernadette
had always been there, but it was silted up. After the child's
obedience had rediscovered it, it started to flow once more,
at first a thin trickle of water, but the next day producing
25,000 gallons of water every twenty-four hours. Miraculous
cures occurred almost at once and have continued for a
century. In 1956, according to the Lourdes archivist,
1,800,000 pilgrims visited it.

Bernadette continued to live in Lourdes for eight years
after the Apparitions. During 1858 and 1859, all witnesses

and all biographers agree that "she was racked by asthma, harassed by crowds, spied upon, admonished, tormented and exhausted". In 1860 she went as a boarder to the Lourdes Hospice of the Sisters of the Order of Charity of Nevers where, though she was more protected, she still had to submit to interviews and examinations. On the feast of the Assumption, 1865, she asked that she might enter the Order and she was allowed to begin her postulancy there at the Lourdes house.

On April 4, 1864, a statue of Our Lady, as Bernadette had seen her, was dedicated and placed in the Grotto. Bernadette was on that occasion confined to the Hospice by illness; but she was able to attend the celebrations in the May of 1866 for the opening of the crypt over which the future chapel was to be built on Massabielle.

She thus stayed in Lourdes long enough to see the carrying out of Our Lady's instructions to her. Six weeks later she left the town to go to the Mother House of the Order at Saint-Gildard, where, on July 29, the feast of St Martha, the patron of the Order, she was received as a novice under her baptismal name of Marie-Bernard. Here she remained till she died a holy death, after intense physical sufferings, on April 16, 1879, aged thirty-five years, three months and nine days.

On August 20, 1908, the feast of St Bernard, the Bishop of Nevers set up an ecclesiastical tribunal to enquire "into the life, the virtues, the reputation for sanctity, and the miracles of the servant of God". In October, 1909, the documents of this first Process were deposited with the Sacred Congregation of Rites. The body of Bernadette was exhumed and found, after thirty years and five months of interment, "shrivelled but entirely complete and without any trace of corruption". It now rests in a crystal shrine in the chapel of Saint-Gildard.

In the August of 1913, the Pope, St Pius X, authorized

the introduction of the cause of canonization. The necessary examination of evidence took twelve years. On June 14, 1925, Pope Pius XI declared Bernadette Blessed. Finally, on a date of appropriate significance—the Feast of the Immaculate Conception in the Holy Year 1933 which commemorated the nineteenth centenary of the Resurrection—Bernadette was canonized.

To see Bernadette as she was during her days in Lourdes is not easy. The blurring of the outline by an eager piety on the one hand and the caricatures of sceptics like Zola on the other have obscured the reality of the Pyrenean girl. Moreover, to the distortions of partisanship have been added the perils of fiction, in particular Franz Werfel's *The Song of Bernadette*, "the one modern book", as Father Martindale has so rightly pointed out, "on which no reliance can be set". A trustworthy contemporary account of her is that contained in the *Annales de la Grotte*, edited by the Garaison Fathers, who knew her well, wished neither to decorate nor to depreciate her and set down with simplicity what they saw. The date of the description is April 1869, three years after she had left Lourdes.

"She was good-natured, gentle, simple and naïve. She was edifying but not extraordinary. She was a child whose wit was rather lacking in versatility and her imagination was somewhat dull. She could not be very talkative. It was not her charm of conversation that won over a whole people to believe in the Apparitions, and no one was more unfitted to arouse enthusiasm. She had no gift of description or power to interest anyone. Her narrative was curt, colourless and cold. You had to keep on questioning her to get a full description of what she had seen. She spoke without any sign of feeling and though she became rather more lively after a time, her joy was never of an ardent kind. She was, indeed, extremely commonplace.

"She appeared to be grave and attentive in her religious practices, but her devotion never rose to the level that many people expected of her after the unheard-of grace of having received eighteen visions."

(One may, perhaps, wonder whether the good Fathers were a little disappointed that grace had not immediately supplanted nature—an attitude also adopted by the Sisters who taught her and disapproved of such harmless school-tricks as throwing her shoe stealthily out of the window on to the strawberry-bed, so that when it was, with permission, reclaimed, an apron-full of strawberries would be introduced into the classroom.)

Grace, moulding nature, was to fashion a saint in God's time; but, as Huysmans has put it, "He took her just as she was, humble and pure, gentle and good, but really 'of no account', to use the very words of the Fathers. He wrought no miracle for her when He raised her at a stroke to Himself. He made no difference between her and her companions and left her a simple *paysanne*".

Bernadette herself had no illusions about her human qualities. That may have been one of the reasons she was chosen. One of the most revealing stories about her, during those days in Lourdes, was how the crowds of women would follow her about, calling her "the little saint". One day, hearing someone say: "If only I could cut off a bit of her dress", she turned round—she who had seen Our Lady —and said, not angrily, but with intense conviction: "How silly you are!"

She could say nothing else. It is only we who, a century after and with more knowledge, may think that, after all, the relic-seeker was not so foolish.

The Particular Circumstances

TIME and place, the unique historical "particularity", are of the essence of the religion of the Incarnation. Wherever they are minimized or forgotten or used ignorantly or lazily as mere symbolism, the edge of truth is blunted. "Bethlehem" itself can come to signify a non-Christian sentimentality, a vaguely beneficent myth, once it has been robbed of the concreteness of the actual over-crowded little town in Judaea in a specific year prescribed for registration by an Imperial edict; and of a certain woman whose child was born there. And "Lourdes", in the course of a century, has acquired many shades of meaning which, though not necessarily untrue, can be misleading if divorced from the questions: Why Bernadette Soubirous? Why Lourdes? Why 1858?

Though the answers, in their fullness, can never be given on earth, that is no excuse for not asking the questions or for not attempting, on the human level, a solution. Indeed, there is a certain obligation to do so. The very circumstance that the story of Bernadette concerns a "private revelation" entails a duty dispassionately to discuss the facts. Any Catholic is as much at liberty as any "free-thinker", if he is genuinely unconvinced by the evidence, to dismiss the story as one of hallucination. Belief is not obligatory, since no revelation having divine authority *can* be imparted since the deaths of the Apostles. As the Holy See is scrupulous to insist, the "authorization" of a "private revelation" means

no more than that nothing in the story is contrary to faith
or morals and that if anyone, after prudently examining the
evidence, considers there are adequate human grounds for
believing it, he is not forbidden to repeat or even to print it.
It remains, in the last analysis, a matter for private judgment,
though, as Father Martindale has put it, "when the Holy
See goes further and applauds a story and enriches it with
prayers and so forth, it would be of the last impertinence for
private students, probably unacquainted with all the
evidence, to disregard it".*

In the case of Bernadette, there is an additional reason for
scrupulous understanding. For Lourdes is, above everything
else, a spectacular challenge. As M. Jean Guitton in *The
Blessed Virgin* has well expressed it, "The stakes are high.
If the Mariophany of Lourdes is authentic, it necessarily
includes and involves the triple edifice of Catholic dogma,
Catholic power and Catholic worship . . . The character of
the debate is anything but academic. For the fact is, to
admit what the vision calls the Immaculate Conception
means admitting the divine motherhood, therefore the
divinity of Christ and the Trinity. It means admitting, too,
the legitimacy of religious development, such as had been
achieved throughout the ages under the headship of the
Bishop of Rome, and especially at that particular point in
1854. It means admitting, as equally valid, what the Vatican
Council defined in 1870 under the term "papal infallibility".
Finally, it means recognizing as legitimate, and approved by
the Spirit of God, the manifestations of popular piety (of
which the Rosary is the most significant form), statues,
chapels (as distinct from parish churches and cathedrals),
pilgrimages and processions, even the *piscina probatica*, the
prayer-grotto, and all the pagan usages sanctified these

---

* It is perhaps worth reminding the reader that a canonization process, involving
the collection, sifting and testing of evidence on every level, provides a *historical*
judgment of unrivalled quality.

twenty centuries by the assimilative power of the Church. It would be hard to find so many truths and practices, all assuming one another and all contained in a clearer symbol: two abstract words, translated into a local dialect, and flowing water. If the truth revealed had been less fundamental, if it had stopped short, for instance, at the Trinity, the apparition would not have involved so many factual implications. So considered, testimony to the Immaculate Conception is a symbol condensing all history: it is like the last word of a novel, explaining and justifying all the preceding twists and turns of the plot".

(I)

The stakes are indeed high; the challenge imperious. And, because of it, it seems almost natural that it should be made by France. It is a commonplace that each of the Catholic nations has its own characteristic virtue to offer as a gift to the Church Universal and that the signature of France is courage. "It is of the very nature of France," as Chesterton perceived, "that the French Catholic should emphasize the fact that the Church is a challenge." And the Frenchman, Charles Péguy, expressed it most memorably in his great poem, *The Mystery of the Charity of Joan of Arc* when he makes the Maid protest, remembering how the disciples forsook Jesus: "Never would the King of France have forsaken him. Never would Charlemagne and Roland; never would the people around here have allowed that to be done. The farrier would have taken his hammer. The women, the poor women, the gleaners would have taken their bill-hooks. Never would Charlemagne and Roland, the men of the Crusades, my Lord Godefroy de Bouillon, never would Saint Louis and even the Lord of Joinville

have forsaken him. Never would our Frenchmen have
renounced him. Never would Saint Denis and Saint Martin,
Saint Genevieve and Saint Aignan, never would Saint
Loup, never would Saint Ouen have forsaken him. Never
would our saints have renounced him. They were saints
who weren't afraid".

And, across the centuries, Bernadette of Lourdes joins
hands with Joan of Domrémy, for Bernadette in spirit is
one of the soldier-saints of France. In the letter she sent to
Pope Pius IX occurs the sentence: "It is some years since I
made myself a little soldier, though an unworthy one, of
Your Holiness". But what she actually wrote in her original
draft before others "improved" it was: "For a long time
now I have been a soldier, though an unworthy one, of
Your Holiness". And the word she used for soldier was
Zouave—the intrepid fighters from the mountain tribes
whose name had, in her lifetime, become a synonym for
courage and loyalty. The difference between the two
versions is that between the real Bernadette and the more
conventional picture of the "little nun".

In 1923, Pope Pius XI, speaking of her virtues, said:
"This life can be summed up in three words: Bernadette
was faithful to her mission: she was humble in glory: she
was valiant under trial". There can have been few better
definitions of the perfect soldier. And she once said of
herself: "If the Blessed Virgin chose me, it was because I
was the most ignorant. She used me as a flint". What she
intended as a humble derogation of her intellect we may
more rightly construe as an apt assessment of her courage.
And because she was, in truth, flint-hard she was able to
become, at an appropriate moment in time and place, Our
Lady's Rock.

At the beginning of it all, everything depended on her.
No one else saw the Vision. Her word, and her word alone,

authenticated it. Her courage and integrity—a poor, backward child of fourteen against the representatives of the Church, the State, the Law and the scientific spirit of the atheist age—safeguarded it until such time as it could be tested and confirmed. Even later, when it had been put beyond all doubt, she herself was the means of converting many who found the miracles ambiguous. If Lourdes, the little town among the Pyrenean foothills, is today a centre of pilgrimage inferior only to Jerusalem and Rome, it is because of Bernadette's militant delivery of Our Lady's message: "I want people to come here in processions" at a time when nobody believed her and even her good parish priest called her a "little liar". And when the circumstances of that time and place are considered, her achievement seems even more remarkable, because, for one thing, her account of the Apparition was only what might have been expected.

(II)

In a ring round Lourdes stand nine hamlets and chapels which were once centres of pilgrimage to Our Lady. The town appears "as a living planet surrounded with nine satellites well-nigh dead". Little is known of some of them— of Notre-Dame de Héas high in the mountains near Barèges: or of the two Notre-Dames de Piétat, the one at Barbazan, the other at Saint-Savin: or of Notre-Dame de Poueylahün at Arrens—but of others the record remains.

The site of Notre-Dame de Nestès, at Montoussé, was said to have been indicated by a sheet of snow falling at midsummer, but the sanctuary had long been abandoned when, in 1848 (Bernadette was four), three little girls saw a luminous statue of Our Lady standing in a thornbush among the ruins. As a result of the vision, the chapel was rebuilt and the ancient statue of Our Lady, which, after the Revolution, had been put in the parish church, was restored to its original place.

Notre-Dame de Médoux, near Bagnères-de-Bigorre, about ten miles from Lourdes, had a more certain history. In 1648, Liloye, a poor shepherdess, had been praying before an historic statue of Our Lady there, when she received from her a message to warn the clergy and people of Bagnères to do penance for their sins. No one took any notice of Liloye who was in consequence given the further message that, unless the people repented, the town would be visited by a plague. In due course the plague came and killed all who could not escape. For a year, Bagnères was deserted. Among those who eventually returned was a certain wealthy woman, Simone de Souville. Meeting Liloye one day, she jeered at her, pointing out that it was only the poor, who had had no means of fleeing from the infection, who had perished.

"Go", said the Blessed Virgin to Liloye, "and warn the black sheep that the scourge shall next smite the rich and that she will be the first to die."

When this prediction was fulfilled to the letter, the people at last repented and year after year processions came to Our Lady's altar. Liloye herself became a nun at Montserrat, but the sanctuary at Médoux was served by Capuchins and became famous for its Pyrenean pilgrimages. Many cures and other miracles occurred there until its destruction by the Revolutionaries, fifty years before Bernadette's birth.

At Bétharram, which is still visited by pilgrims to Lourdes, the original shrine was burnt down by the Protestants in 1569; it was restored in 1616. On the eve of the Assumption, 1622, a fountain, which had for years been dried up, inexplicably started to flow in a little grotto near the church. Many miracles of healing occurred in this water. In the church a bas-relief memorialized the story of the original choice of the place by an appearance to shepherd boys of Our Lady, smiling, in a burning bush.

It was, however, the story of Notre-Dame de Garaison which provided the closest anticipation of Lourdes. At the beginning of the sixteenth century, at a place in the vale of Garaison known as "Goat's Moor", because it was the traditional meeting-place of the witches and sorcerers of Gascony, a young shepherdess named Anglèse was tending her father's flocks near a spring when a Lady, clothed in white, appeared to her. Announcing that she was the Blessed Virgin, she asked for a chapel to be built there and processions made. No one believed the girl's story, but Anglèse returned twice more to the place. On both occasions she saw the Lady, though her family and some friends who accompanied her did not. To overcome their unbelief, the Lady said that she would change the piece of black bread in the girl's bag, as well as what was stored in the bread-bin at home, into white loaves. The other people, though they still could not see the Apparition, heard these words and, as both miracles took place, immediately discarded their disbelief. The chapel was built and, at the statue of Our Lady of Sorrows which was installed in it, so many conversions and cures occurred that by 1536 a vast church had to be built to house the crowds which came from all parts of France.

During the Wars of Religion, the church was plundered by the Protestants and the statue thrown on the fire. But it was not destroyed and when peace was once more restored it was again set in place. Garaison became again the goal of pilgrimage and was, indeed, to the sixteenth and seventeenth centuries very much what Lourdes is to this. But the prosperity thus brought to the town led to avarice and licentiousness and Our Lady withdrew. At the Revolution, the church was turned into a powder-factory, but in 1834 (ten years

B

before Bernadette's birth) the Bishop of Tarbes restored the sanctuary and, in order to serve it, founded an association of missionaries from which came the Fathers of Lourdes.

Thus, as J. K. Huysmans put it in *The Crowds of Lourdes*, "Lourdes is not an isolated instance in the annals of the Pyrenees. It is but the revival of old popular devotions which have been rejuvenated by the Madonna: without any change of district, she has restricted herself to transferring her abode to a site within easier reach of the devotion of crowds".

Whether or not Bernadette herself knew of these shrines and their stories, it is quite certain that the ecclesiastical authorities (in particular the Bishop of Tarbes) were acquainted with them. And their knowledge makes their initial distrust of Bernadette eminently explicable.

(III)

There were other circumstances which might tend to increase scepticism. It was difficult to separate, in thought, the appearances of Our Lady to Catherine Labouré in 1830 from those to Bernadette in 1858, at least in so far as they both concerned the Immaculate Conception.

In the Mother House of the Sisters of Charity in Paris on the night of July 18, 1830, a twenty-four-year-old nun of the order, Catherine Labouré, had been awakened by a beautiful child about five years old, who said: "Come to the chapel; the Blessed Virgin is waiting for you". She had obeyed, followed the child and found in the chapel the altar candles lighted as if for midnight Mass. There she had been greeted by a Lady, wearing a yellow dress and a blue cloak, sitting on the left side of the sanctuary in the place usually occupied by the Director of the Community.

On November 27, in the same year, Sister Catherine again saw the Lady in the chapel. This time she was dressed in a gold-coloured gown, very plain and high-necked. Her head was covered with a white veil, which floated over her shoulders down to her feet. Her feet rested on a globe and she held another globe in her hands. "Suddenly her fingers were covered with rings of precious stones. Rays of dazzling light darted from them and the whole of her figure was enveloped in such radiance that her feet and dress were no longer visible . . . After a while an oval frame surrounded the Blessed Virgin on which was written in letters of gold: 'O Mary, conceived without sin, pray for us who have recourse to thee'. Then a voice said to me," records Sister Catherine, " 'Get a medal struck after this model; those who wear it when it is blessed will receive great graces.' "

The oval frame slowly revolved. On the back of it was the letter "M", surmounted by a cross with a cross-bar beneath it, and under all the Sacred Hearts of Jesus and Mary, the former surrounded by a crown of thorns, the latter pierced by a sword.

Sister Catherine's confessor was sceptical about the authenticity of the vision and the message; but a few weeks later, Our Lady appeared again, this time looking about forty years old and standing above the tabernacle, and again made her request.

The matter was then thoroughly considered and in 1832, with the approval of the Archbishop of Paris, the first "Miraculous Medal", propagating belief in the Immaculate Conception, was struck. In 1847 Pope Pius IX allowed the establishment of a Confraternity of the Immaculate Conception, whose members were known as the Children of Mary and whose badge was the Miraculous Medal.

Bernadette herself was one of the Children of Mary in Lourdes. She actually compared Our Lady as she appears on the Medal with the Apparition in the Grotto, explaining that *her* Lady held her hands in the same position as shown on the Miraculous Medal, "but it hadn't got that in its hands"—the "that" being the rays of light represented by a fan-arrangement of lines. The statue of Our Lady of the Miraculous Medal was the first one to be put in the niche of the Apparition. And on the evening of the first Apparition, before she went to bed, Bernadette finished her rosary with "O Mary, conceived without sin, pray for us who have recourse to thee", as usual. But this time, as she said it, she went pale, as she had at the Grotto, and burst into tears.

Some writers have assumed that it was at this moment she first realized intuitively who her Lady was. Whether this were so or whether, as others have suggested, she was merely tired and overwrought, there can be no doubt that she made no conscious connection with "the Immaculate Conception", for proofs are overwhelming that she did not understand the phrase, even when Our Lady herself used it. But it is easy to see, in the circumstances, why the ecclesiastical authorities were inclined to suspect, at the very least, some theological "prompting".

In 1846, sixteen years after the appearance to Catherine Labouré and twelve years before that to Bernadette, Our Lady is said to have appeared to two children near La Salette on the heights of the Alps in Southern France. On September 19, at three o'clock in the afternoon in full sunlight, Mélanie Calvat, a shepherdess of fifteen, and Maximin Giraud, a shepherd boy of eleven, saw, surrounded by a great light, a "beautiful lady" dressed in a strange costume, who, speaking alternately in French and in the local patois, charged them with a message to deliver "to all her people".

This message contained no reference to herself or to her Immaculate Conception but was confined to a denunciation of the sins of Christendom, a call to penance and a warning of punishment unless amendment followed. Before disappearing she confided to each child a special secret. She did not appear again.

The bishop of the diocese ordered an investigation, as a result of which the reality of the apparition was admitted. Pilgrimages started. Cures were wrought at the spring at the place where the Lady had appeared; but the difficulty of communications and the impossibility of hauling the sick and infirm by the tortuous mountain tracks to a height of over 5,000 feet led to a gradual abandonment of pilgrims' visits. The decline was aided both by the scepticism of the natives of the region and by the doubts of many of the faithful. Though at the end of 1851 the bishop of the diocese authorized the cult of Our Lady of La Salette, the attacks continued to such an extent that he resigned his office. The sceptics claimed that the "beautiful lady" was in fact identifiable as a young woman named Lamerlière—which led to "a widely-advertised suit for slander". Nevertheless, in 1852, the first stone of a great church was solemnly laid on the site of the appearance, which was to become the mother church of the Missionaries of La Salette, now dedicated throughout the world to combating the sins denounced in the Vision's discourse.*

* Since the subject of La Salette bristles with difficulties, it may be permissible to quote from the *Catholic Encyclopedia* the conclusion of the matter as far as it concerns the two children, whose subsequent lives provide a relevant contrast with that of Bernadette. The two secrets, which neither child told the other, were, on the advice of the bishop, sent to the Pope in 1851. "It is unknown what impression these mysterious revelations made on the Pope, for on this point there are two versions diametrically opposed to each other. Maximin's secret is not known for it was never published. Mélanie's was inserted in its entirety in a brochure which she herself had printed in 1879 at Lecce, Italy, with the approval of the bishop of that town. A lively controversy followed as to whether the secret published in 1879 was identical with that communicated to Pius IX in 1851, or whether in its second form it was not merely a work of the imagination. The latter was the opinion of wise and prudent persons, who were persuaded that a distinction must be made between the two Mélanies, between the innocent and simple *voyante* of 1846 and the visionary of 1879, whose mind had been disturbed by reading apocalyptic books and the lives of *illuminati*. As Rome uttered no decision, the strife was prolonged between the disputants. Most of the defenders of the text of 1879 suffered censure from their bishops. Maximin Giraud, after an unhappy and wandering life, returned to his native village and there died a holy death (1st March, 1875). Mélanie Calvat ended a no less wandering life at Altamura on 15th December, 1904.

At the same time as the controversy about the authenticity of the Vision of La Salette—in 1850 and 1851— considerable publicity in both the Catholic and the non-Catholic Press in France was being given to the disturbing case of Rose Tamisier. Rose was a young and sickly peasant girl who claimed to have been favoured with supernatural visions. She declared that celestial hands had administered the Blessed Sacrament to her and that, on certain days, she bore marks of the Stigmata. In the church where she worshipped a picture, representing the Descent from the Cross, seemed to bear witness to her claims. Where the wounds of Christ were painted on the canvas, thick blood oozed, in the first place while she was praying there alone, later in the presence of a crowd of people who immediately proclaimed it a miracle.

The Archbishop of Avignon, in whose diocese these events occurred, instituted enquiries, which eventually proved the girl to be a fraud, in complicity with the sacristan and the parish priest. She was sentenced to a term of imprisonment.

This case was still sufficiently in everyone's mind during the events at Lourdes seven years later, for M. Falconnet, the Chief Imperial Prosecutor, reporting on Bernadette to his Minister, to write: "The judicial authorities kept a close watch on the affair, seeking, but not finding, an occasion to intervene. The situation was not comparable with the affair of Rose Tamisier, who deliberately staged a miracle. In the present case the child is simply suffering from an hallucination. She really believes that she has seen something".

It should be clear enough why the Church in 1858 had to take even greater precautions than the lay officials. Her attitude might be summed up by the Abbé Peyramale, the parish priest of Lourdes, in two sentences which, though not uttered on the same occasion, are complementary. "We do not yet know whether it is a miracle, imagination or deceit: we must wait" and "Be assured, my friends, that the gates of Hell will not prevail against that which God proposes to establish." It was this necessary scepticism (expressed, for instance, unkindly in a nun's remark to Bernadette: "If it *is* Our Lady, you had better ask her to help you learn your catechism") that provided a greater test of her courage than the attacks and questioning of the atheists. She had to be suspected by those who might have been expected to—and of course, eventually did—defend her. She had to be wounded in the house of her friends.

One can see, also, looking back from the vantage-point of today, what may be one of the reasons for Our Lady's choice of Bernadette and Lourdes, which is logically intelligible on the human and historical plane.

(IV)

The nineteenth century was to see the assault on Christianity intensified in at least two new ways. First, there were to be the discoveries of natural science which, by a false philosophy, could be used by enemies of the Faith to turn the vast body of the indolent, the illiterate and the "intellectuals" against the Church. Secondly, there was to be a rise of "modernism", with an accompanying apparatus of Biblical criticism, which tended to reduce the Christ of the Gospels to a human level.

Cardinal Newman, then the Anglican Vicar of St. Mary's, Oxford, had foreseen, in a sermon preached in 1838, something of what might happen in the scientific world. Speaking of the "miracles" which were a sign of Antichrist, he said: "Whether real miracles or not, whether pretended, or the result, as some have conjectured, of discoveries in physical science, they will produce the same effect as if they were real, namely the overpowering the imaginations of such as have not the love of God deeply lodged in their hearts—of all but the elect". He added: "Scripture is remarkably precise and consistent in this prediction" and instances as one of the New Testament warnings a prophecy of St John, which may sound less puzzling today than in 1838: "He doeth great wonders so that he maketh fire come down from heaven on the earth in the sight of men, and deceiveth them that dwell on the earth by the means of those miracles which he had power to do in the sight of the Beast".

In our own day a Frenchman, Jacques Maritain, has epitomized in a sentence the root of the *malaise* of the last hundred years: "The error of the modern world and the modern mind consists in the claim to ensure the domination of nature by reason while at the same time refusing the domination of reason by supernature".

And one may be permitted to ask whether it was altogether a coincidence that the last appearance of Our Lady to Bernadette, unexpected and out of sequence, was made a fortnight after Charles Darwin had delivered in London his famous paper which, the following year, was to be enlarged and published as *The Origin of Species*? And that the date she chose was the Feast of Our Lady of Mount Carmel, commemorating that day, July 16, 1251, when she had stood on English grass, in the Priory of Aylesford in Kent, and made her wishes known to Simon Stock, an English saint?

On July 16, 1858, in Lourdes, it will be remembered, the Grotto had been closed and a barrier erected across it by the temporarily triumphant forces of scientific scepticism, so that Bernadette had to kneel far away in the field across the river. When they asked her, "How could you see the

Vision from La Ribière? The river is so wide there and the barrier so high?" she answered: "I saw neither the river nor the boards of the barrier. I only saw the Blessed Virgin; but never had I seen her look so lovely".

Since we are living in the midst of the scientific developments which have not yet reached their end, there is no need to insist on the difference between the real miracles at Lourdes—ordinary water with no intrinsic curative properties healing in an instant diseases which all the resources of medical science have failed to touch—and the "miracles" arising from man's pride and curiosity, used for his selfish ends and implicit with horror, suffering and destruction on an unimaginable scale. In this sense, the challenge of Lourdes is too obvious to emphasize. But the theological implications of modernism, in preparing a climate for intellectual infidelity, are also relevant.

It has been wisely said that any good man, whatever his religion, can agree with the Sermon on the Mount (which, as the Sermon was a summary of the highest moral precepts and acknowledged ethical conduct to which man had attained by his natural powers, is to be expected). Any man who believes in God, however "God" be defined, can join in the *Our Father*. But the test of the Christian, separating him from all others, is the *Hail Mary*. It is the *Hail Mary* which still announces the Incarnation.

From at least the fifth century, when Our Lady was defined as Mother of God as an answer to the influential heresy attacking Our Lord's divinity, every Catholic had understood the simple dogmatic fact which underlay it: Mary is literally and truly the Mother of Jesus; therefore He is true man. Jesus is true God, therefore she is the Mother of God. As Mary was the human instrument of the Incarnation, so, through the ages, she has been the defender of its truth. "Today, as in the fifth century, in London as at Ephesus,

the honour of Mary is the safeguard, the outpost of the
Adoration of her Son."

As the attacks on the divinity of Jesus Christ grew more
subtle, so their results in practice led to increasing confusion.
Not only outside the Church, but even within it, powerful
intellects interpreted Christian truths in a diminished sense.
The situation has been simply, though adequately, described
thus: "This system (modernism) allowed its exponents,
while professing belief in Christ, to deny any other than a
symbolic truth to any article of the Creed concerning Him.
His Virgin Birth, His Resurrection, were declared, as
phenomenal facts, to belong not to religion but to history,
and as such to be judged, approved or condemned, while as
dogmas they were true with the truth of symbols".*

The modernists were, of course, answered in the Encyclical
Pascendi and their leaders excommunicated—a proceeding
which led to "the usual outcry of 'tyranny, obscurantism,
bigotry' from the non-Catholic world: every journal
professing rigid adherence to the 'three historic Creeds'
hastened in their hatred of Rome to condone the offence of
those whom Rome condemned for undermining all
Creeds"—but the positive answer was to define more
exactly, as matters of faith, the nature of Our Lady.

The saying that "all heresies are brought to nothing by
Mary" is seen as particularly true in this context. The whole
of Protestant thought, adopting modernist criticism, had
found a way of emptying the Creeds of all meaning (though
its exponents found the *Quicunque Vult*, the "Athanasian
Creed", unexpectedly difficult to "get round" and conse-
quently, during the nineteenth century, tried to abolish it
from confessions of faith). Non-Catholic Christians could
still proclaim an allegiance to "Christ". They could still
profess a belief in the "Incarnation" in a symbolic sense.

* M. L. Cozens, *A Handbook of Heresies*: Modernism.

But they could not meet the challenge of Mary. They could not—and do not—accept those rigidly defining dogmas of the nature of Christ and the Incarnation which are known as the Immaculate Conception and the Glorious Assumption.

After the definition of the *Theotokos*, the Mother of God, there was, for fifteen centuries, no need for further official utterance. Within the Church, of course, thought about Our Lady and devotion to her were constant among the theologians and the simple alike; and by the end of the Middle Ages the dogma of the Immaculate Conception, which was universally believed, could have been made *de fide*. The Church, however, contented herself with forbidding any public attack upon it. In her wisdom, she waited until the moment appropriate for defining it as an article of Faith. And it was Our Lady herself who made the moment known.

(v)

Against this background, the sequence of events leading up to Lourdes becomes inescapably significant—the appearance to Catherine Labouré in 1830, with the request for the distribution of the "Miraculous Medal" to "popularize", so to speak, the Immaculate Conception, followed, in due time, in 1854, by the Pope's "infallible" definition of the dogma; then the crucial appearance in 1858 to Bernadette: "I am the Immaculate Conception" confirming the definition and establishing by miracles at her chosen shrine at Lourdes a climate in which the original definition of 1854 could be re-emphasized by the further definition, in 1870, of "infallibility" itself.

She appeared in Lourdes at a moment when, because of

false visionaries and the eclipse of La Salette, a revivification of belief was most needed. And however one may interpret La Salette, none can gainsay the dramatic contrast between the characters of Mélanie and Bernadette. One need only instance the difference between Mélanie's treatment of her "secret" and Bernadette's answer to those who enquired: "If His Holiness the Pope were to ask you to tell him the Lady's secrets what would you do?"—"I should say to His Holiness that they were the Lady's secrets and then he wouldn't ask me any more to tell him".

And, in her appearance at Lourdes, Our Lady was returning not only to a district already associated with her but in a manner which repeated the signs she had already given at neighbouring shrines. She was gracious enough, one might say, to give the known passwords.

There are, however, other reasons for the appropriateness of Lourdes.

II

The Place

(1)

LOURDES, with its river and its rock, has been inhabited as long as history, and prehistoric remains have been found in its caves. The rock, at the junction of three valleys, has been from Roman times the site for a castle which has dominated the countryside, a strong point for the *Château Fort* which has given its holders the strategic command of an important region. For that reason, it has been a continuing battle ground since at least the time when the Roman eagles were set up there after Julius Caesar's conquest of Gaul and the Roman engineers built the Old Bridge across the river. The Visigoths, the Saracens and the Franks occupied and held it. During the Hundred Years' War, it was in English hands for forty-six years. It was a prize which fell in turn, during the French Wars of Religion, to Huguenots and Catholics.

Its very name, according to the accepted derivation, is one which, dating from the eighth century, proclaims it Our Lady's domain. In 732, Charles Martel defeated the invading Saracens at Tours in that battle which was a turning point in the history of the world because on its, issue depended whether Christian civilization should continue or Mohammedanism become the religion of Europe.

In their retreat to Spain, which they held, the Saracens conquered and kept a certain number of regional outposts, including the important Castle of Mirambel on the rock of

19

Lourdes. They had held it for forty-six years when, in 778, Charlemagne besieged it on his return through the Pyrenean passes from his campaign against the Saracens in Spain, immortalized in the Song of Roland. The commander, the Mohammedan Mirat, had sworn that he would never yield to any mortal man and with notable bravery held out to the point of starvation. The chaplain of Charlemagne's army, Roricius, Bishop of Le Puy, at last managed to obtain an audience with him and—it is said—spoke thus: "Brave prince, you have sworn never to yield to any mortal man. Could you not with honour make your surrender to an immortal lady, Mary, Queen of Heaven?"

As Bishop of Le Puy, Roricius was guardian of the greatest shrine of Our Lady in France. She had appeared there to a sick widow in the third century and, since then, continuous pilgrimages had been made to its famous statue of the Blessed Virgin, venerated as Notre-Dame de France. Charlemagne himself twice made the pilgrimage and six years before the expedition to Spain, had granted the cathedral special privileges because of its outstanding sanctity and fame.

Roricius was, therefore, in a position to be able to say to Mirat that, as guardian of the seat of Our Lady in the west —"She has her throne at Le Puy and I am her humble minister there"—he could accept, in her name, the Mohammedan chief's submission. In token of his vassalage, Mirat agreed to take to the sanctuary of his Queen at Le Puy a handful of grass plucked from the banks of the Gave. He was baptized under the name of Lorus (which is the derivation of Lourdes) and, as a Christian, knighted by Charlemagne, he remained in command of the fort.

Lourdes was thus dedicated to Our Lady in a very special way—was, in fact, Our Lady's fief—from the eighth century; and the outward and visible sign of that connection was the "grass" which Bernadette was so mysteriously bidden to eat when the Queen of Heaven visited Lourdes eleven centuries later.*

As Lourdes had been a battle-ground in the most literal sense from its earliest history, it seems appropriate enough that it should become in due time a battle-ground for the Faith—not least because many of the wars had involved the Faith itself. The castle had been occupied in turn by the exponents of all the great heresies. On the town had been imposed the paganism of Rome and the Arianism of the Visigoths, the Mohammedanism of the Saracens and the Calvinism of the Huguenots before in Bernadette's day it was chosen to try conclusions with the scientific modernism which, because it attacked the very roots of all dogmatic theology, was the deadliest heresy of all. And still, behind the simple piety of the Catholics and the "discreet" scepticism of the "liberals" in club and café, there were influences from the far past, ancient superstitions, which had still to be defeated.

(II)

Massabielle, the Old Rock (*masse vieille*), in which was the cave of the spring and the niche of Our Lady's appearance, was a place of superstition and dread. The Lourdais

---

* During those centuries, the development at Le Puy, because of its connection with Lourdes, is worth noting. At the end of the eleventh century a Bishop of Le Puy composed the *Salve Regina*. St Louis IX, returning from his crusade, gave to the cathedral an ebony image of Our Lady—"the Black Virgin"—a copy of which was given to Lourdes and is, today, in the Castle. Pilgrimages by the Kings of France to Notre-Dame de France were constant. Among the many exclusive privileges accorded to it was the right of the bishop to wear the *pallium*, reserved for archbishops and, in the Bull granting this, the Pope announced :"Nowhere does the Blessed Virgin receive a more special and a more filial worship", with the result that the Cathedral of Le Puy assumed a sort of primacy among the churches of France and even of Christendom. It was defended against the attack of the Huguenots in 1562 by priests and religious who, for this occasion, were permitted to arm themselves; but, in 1793, the Revolutionaries tore the statue from its shrine and burnt it in the public square. In 1860, not long before the beginning of work for the site of the chapel at Lourdes, there was dedicated at Le Puy a colossal statue of 'Notre-Dame de France' made from more than 200 cannon captured at the battle of Sebastopol which had been given to the bishop by Napoleon III.

avoided it. A favourite haunt of wild swine and snakes, it was used only by occasional shepherds, sheltering from storms. In all probability, it had been a place of pre-Christian rites and worship (for the spring had always been there, though it was now silted up and unknown). When Bernadette first told the story of the Lady's appearance in that place, her mother immediately concluded that it was the Devil and twice said so. That was, indeed, her reason for prohibiting Bernadette from revisiting Massabielle; and when permission was at last given for a return, it was only on condition that, should the Vision reappear, it was to be sprinkled with holy water, so that if it were a manifestation of the diabolic or the Devil himself in one of his metamorphoses, it would be rendered harmless. And when Bernadette did throw holy water at the Vision, it will be remembered, Our Lady smiled in approval, bowed her head and made the sign of the Cross. The precaution was approved.

The implications of the diabolism and paganism associated with the Grotto recur throughout the story and, though some writers minimize or even omit them, they are important to the understanding of it; for the "Christianizing" of Massabielle is the first chapter in the tale of Lourdes.

The worship of natural forces, especially the waters springing from the earth which provided man with a very necessity of life, is one of the oldest manifestations of religion. Indians, Egyptians, Persians, Greeks, Romans all had deities of their springs and streams. In Lourdes itself, during its Roman days, the festival of Fontinalia, in honour of the nymphs of wells and fountains, would have been observed on October 13. The place of pilgrimage may even have been the spring at Massabielle and the old Roman bridge, over which Bernadette went to the Grotto, may have borne the feet of those going to celebrate the Fontinalia fifteen hundred years before.

How strong was the people's devotion to this worship is evidenced by the early Christian missionaries all over Europe who "Christianized" and dedicated to a saint so many existing springs and wells to which veneration had, from time immemorial, been paid. How superficial, in many cases, was the "conversion" is suggested by the fact that the Council of Tours in 567 interdicted the custom of idolatrous worship at springs and that, even in 1102, St Anselm had to direct: "Let no one attribute reverence or sanctity to a fountain, without the Bishop's authority". Gildas could write of the fountains and the rivers, "now subservient to the use of men, but which once were an abomination to them and to which the blind people paid divine honour". Though sacrifices to springs were probably unknown, as a general rule, in the nineteenth century, a certain amount of superstition lingered on—as it does today—and long after Bernadette's time curious customs survived by which young girls in the Pyrenees told their own fortunes in spring waters on the morning of May-day.

Without entering into the deeper anthropological questions, one can admit also the same significances in Holy Writ, from the days of Moses who made water flow from the rock to the pool of Bethesda, the *piscina probatica*, by which Jesus stood in Jerusalem. Nor, one may think, is it merely a coincidence that the Gospel appointed to be read at Mass on the day after Our Lady pointed out to Bernadette the spring at Massabielle was precisely that which records how "in Jerusalem, by the sheep-market, was a pool which in Hebrew was called Bethesda, having five porches. In these lay a great number of impotent folk, of blind, halt, withered, waiting for the moving of the water; for an angel went down at a certain season into the pool; whosoever then first after the troubling of the water stepped in was made whole of whatsoever disease he had".

c

The sequence of events in that February of 1858 had an exact pattern—the finding of the spring, followed the next morning by the reading of that Gospel at Mass, the liturgical reminder by the Church, followed either that evening or the next day by the first of the miraculous cures at the spring, the giving of sight to the blind stonemason.

But the earlier days had an equally strict sequence and if the logic of it was not necessarily apparent to the nineteenth-century Lourdais, it would have been immediately recognizable to the early Christian missionaries who were notably aware of "the ancient gods pursuing" and the imperative of exorcism.

On the first day of the "great fortnight"—the fortnight which Our Lady asked Bernadette to visit the Grotto every day—Bernadette revealed how she had heard behind her loud yells, like a thousand angry people shouting—"confused voices shrieking at each other, clashing together". One voice, more furious than the rest, dominated them all and roared out: "Get out of here! Get out of here!" She guessed rightly that the curses and threats were directed, not at her, but at the Vision. Our Lady merely glanced in the direction from which they came. "This single look", as Mgr Trochu puts it, "one of sovereign authority, reduced the invisible mob to silence. The enemy of all good would not drive her from the Grotto where she gave her audiences".

The driving of the Devil from his ancient fastness was, therefore, the first action of the fortnight. But though "at Massabielle, the future was to prove that the Spirit of Evil, in this burst of fury, had admitted his defeat", certain minor manifestations continued for months. There was what can only be described as an epidemic of false visionaries, "some of them obviously manipulated by occult forces, others the sport of their own temperament whose weaknesses could be exploited by Satan for his perverse ends . . . There were fanatics, exhibitionists, lying maniacs, hysterics, half-wits, with a few tricksters thrown in ... To disentangle human trickery from the devil's deceits in all this would be more than a little difficult. In every case, a point of the utmost importance stands out clearly : The suspect apparitions never showed themselves in the niche ".

It will be enough to instance two examples. The Lourdes hairdresser's twelve-year-old son who, like Bernadette, was in the First Communion class, was one day standing in the front of the Grotto when he saw coming towards him and apparently issuing from the rock itself, "a lady all in gold and covered with furbelows". She had her hands and the lower part of her body hidden in an ash-coloured cloud like a storm-cloud. "She fixed me with her big black eyes and seemed to want to nab me. I immediately thought it was the Ugly One (the Devil) and so I ran away." While he was telling this, "the child was shaking all over and clinging desperately to his mother's skirts".

Another manifestation which was witnessed by many of the Lourdais concerned a young farm-worker "of ungainly appearance". He would visit the Grotto alone on certain days and, as soon as he drew near it, he had a sort of seizure, starting to spin round at a giddy speed, like a dancing dervish. When he stopped, he would look up in the air and appeared to try to catch some invisible being above him in his hands. During this manoeuvre he would rise several feet up the face of the rock and remain there, levitated. On returning to normal, the young man appeared bewildered, and, in extreme despondency, ran away. When questioned he said that he had no control of his will and that some secret power, operating from inside the rocks, compelled him to act as he did.

One of the immediate consequences of these diabolic manifestations was to throw doubt on Bernadette herself.

Brother Léobard, the schoolmaster, who taught the frightened son of the hairdresser as well as Bernadette, later admitted: "I regarded all this as sheer farce and I came to have very grave doubts about Bernadette's visions, at which I had never been present". His absence, of course, was due to the Abbé Peyramale's order that none of his clergy was to go to the Grotto lest, by their presence, they should seem to give the Church's approval to a matter which was still undecided. But, though there is no reason to suppose that Brother Léobard was in the least unorthodox, his phrasing suggests that he saw nothing but human trickery in the various manifestations. In the mid-nineteenth century it was sometimes difficult, even in the Church, to escape the unconscious bias of rationalism.

Satan always seems to have it both ways. As Baudelaire was at that moment pointing out, the Devil's best trick is to convince men that he does not exist. By this means, not only can he work unobserved, but the convenient disbelief can be applied to and include all supernatural existence, including God. The "free-thinking" bourgeoisie of Lourdes could argue either that, as the diabolic manifestations were, *ex hypothesi*, only some kind of explicable force or human trickery, therefore Bernadette's visions were of the same kind; or, alternatively, that if there *should* be anything in this superstition of the supernatural, it was a "power" without moral implications which put the "apes of Bernadette" and Bernadette herself on the same level. Mesmerism and catalepsy were the fashionable explanations.

Above all, it was an age of progress and since the Reformation "more or less admittedly, there is present in the notion of progress the idea that the world can do without God, because it is itself God".* The theology of such a

---

* The true notion of progress is suggested by Chesterton's saying: "Progress is a sacred word, a word that could only rightly be used by rigid believers and in the ages of Faith".

world was Pelagianism, the essential error of which is that
it denies the need for redemption and binds God within the
limits of nature as we experience it. All that is needed is to
change the conditions of man's life, urge him to use his
free will and humanity will save itself. And as Bishop Gore
has memorably epitomized it: "The Nestorian Christ is the
fitting Saviour of the Pelagian man". It was the Nestorian
heresy, it will be remembered, which called forth the
definition of the Theotokos, of Mary as Mother of God.
From its constricted, two-dimensional world, Pelagianism,
the religion of progress, banishes Mary, as well as God—
and the Devil. And so, in some sense, when in God's good
time Mary asserted herself and the impact of reality shattered
the make-believe of rationalism in Lourdes, it was only to be
expected that the Devil, too, would be forced into the open
and would manifest himself in his own person.

(III)

In this battle, Bernadette herself had a vital part to play.
If, at the Great Exorcism, she was protected by Our Lady
herself, it was, in the days to come, her own attitude and
bearing which convinced the Lourdais that there was nothing in common between her and the other "visionaries".

If Brother Léobard, like the Abbé Peyramale's curates,
was unable to form his own judgment, the Abbé Dézirat, a
visitor not under the Lourdes jurisdiction, was unaffected
by the ban. He, too, was "inclined to think they [Bernadette's
visions] were illusions" and decided to see for himself.

"From the moment Bernadette appeared," he wrote, "I
watched her closely; her face was calm, her appearance
modest and her walk natural, neither slow nor hurried.
There was no trace of excitement or sickness: everything

about her showed that here was a sane mind in a healthy body." At the Grotto itself, where there was an enormous crowd, a way was made for him and he was able to stand, at most, a yard from Bernadette. "I was determined to see and to see clearly, so I put on my spectacles, which were very good ones! My whole attention was on the child's face: my eyes were glued to her and I never looked away for an instant . . . Bernadette hardly moved her lips, as she told her beads. The expression of her face and her whole attitude showed that her soul was in ecstasy. It reflected the deepest peace and the most profound contemplation. It is impossible to give you an idea of her smile."

(This smile, which seems to have mirrored that of Our Lady, has become so much a part of the story of Bernadette that it is worth interpolating here an incident which happened later when she was a postulant. A tourist called at the Hospice, hoping to see her "for the fun of the thing". As it happened, she opened the door to him and when he explained his reason for calling she said: "I am Bernadette".

"Oh, you are the girl who sees the Blessed Virgin," he said. "It's all lies, of course, but, just the same, could you tell me what you see?"

"As you wouldn't believe me, that would be useless."

"At least show me how she smiled. I'm a great sinner and perhaps that smile might convert me!"

"That smile is seen only in Heaven. I could never show it to you. But, as you are a sinner, I will do what I can."

The tourist turned away to hide his confusion and left the place a changed man.)

To return to the Abbé Dézirat: "The purity, gentleness and love which shone in her eyes as she gazed on the Vision captivated me as much as her smile; so did the joy and sorrow which passed over her face in turn. The joy was the joy of Heaven; the sorrow sharp as a two-edged sword and deep as an abyss, yet neither the one nor the other disturbed her peace. They succeeded each other with the speed of lightning but there was nothing harsh or abrupt in the change. I cannot tell you how this was so, and I am sure that the most gifted author would fail miserably were he to attempt to do so".

When he was cross-examined on this part of his narrative, the question was asked: "Did you notice Bernadette tremble?" He answered: "No. While the periods of joy lasted it seemed as though a light was shining in the child's face; during the grief a kind of veil seemed to cover it. You would have said that her soul withdrew itself, as though weighed down by unspeakable sorrow".

The Abbé's narrative concluded: "I took in every detail of the child's appearance when she arrived at the Grotto, and I can only say that the difference between what she was then and what I saw at the time of the Apparition was the difference between matter and spirit. The crowd itself was overwhelmed by emotion. Only Bernadette saw the Apparition but everyone felt the Presence. This was obvious from the silence, respect and recollection which reigned everywhere. A strange mixture of joy and fear was on every face. It was good to be there: I thought I was in the ante-chamber of Heaven".

Finally, in reply to the question: "What are your general impressions?" he said: "I was ashamed to set foot in such a holy place. I was convinced—most profoundly convinced—of the reality of the Vision".

(IV)

There is one other matter which, it seems to me, may well be connected with the exorcism of the Devil. I put this

forward tentatively and as a purely personal opinion; and I
do not suggest that, even if it be true, it constitutes the full
explanation of Our Lady's command to Bernadette to eat
the "grass" (which was in fact a bitter-tasting herb) by the
spring. That, on the human and historical plane, it had some
connection with the tribute which Mirat had paid when he
surrendered the castle of Lourdes to Our Lady, seems
sufficiently obvious. But it may have had a deeper significance on the sacramental level.

The material Our Lord chose for the Sacrament of His
Body and Blood was bread and wine, not wheat and grapes.
The natural gifts which men took from the bounty of the
earth had to be transformed by their labour before they were
a fit subject for transubstantiation into the Body and Blood
of God. There is no need to enter here into all the implication of this theological truism, except to point out that
bread and wine, as they truly represent the necessity and the
joy of life, are valid symbols for a working and sacrificing
humanity and can thus be rightly offered for the divine
acceptance, change and return as the food of immortality.

To offer only the fruits of the earth would be to repeat
the mistake of Cain, whose vegetable sacrifice which in the
last analysis cost him nothing, was rejected by God. And,
just as the Cainites who claimed Cain as their prophet
became one of the Gnostic sects which made a deadly
assault on Christianity in its early years, so in the various
later manifestations of paganism and heresy, the partaking
of water and grasses or wild herbs became at worst a
parody of the Sacrament and at best the survival of an
intelligible aspect of nature worship.

The example which immediately comes to my mind is
connected with the death of William Rufus. The King was
a bitter and avowed anti-Christian, though the exact nature
of his belief—whether neo-Gnosticism, Catharism or a

simple paganism—is difficult to determine. In the accounts of his end, written by initiates of his own cult who were scrupulous to preserve the meaning of it, it was said that he was killed in a pre-Christian holy place after partaking a kind of last sacrament of herbs and flowers. (The date was two years before Anselm's edict, to which reference has been made, prohibiting worship at springs.)

If, then, Massabielle was to be "Christianized", Our Lady's command to Bernadette to perform in obedience to her and in a spirit of profound humility, the action of drinking the spring water, and eating the herb might be the last stage of the exorcism. It would be in line with the whole of Christian action from the earliest missionary days, which reinterpreted and "sanctified" the usages of an innocent paganism or of an honest, if mistaken, belief, and dedicated them to the service of God. The action is so completely congruous with the rest of the revelation that it adds the final touch of authenticity. Had there been only the re-discovery of a silted-up spring, there might still on one level have been a loophole for ambiguity. Because of the eating of the "grass", there is none.

(v)

The Devil's attacks did not, of course, end with the sanctification of Massabielle; but they assumed their more normal form, which they have kept to this day. On the very day of the Great Exorcism, the evening edition of the local anti-clerical paper, *Lavedan*, invented its own version of circumstances which had taken Bernadette to the Grotto: "Three young children went to collect dead branches, the debris of wood-cutting just outside the town. The girls were surprised by the owner of the land and they fled as fast as their legs could carry them into one of the grottos by the forest road . . ."

From that day continued the stream of lies and distortions to find what some may consider its climax, months later, in the conclusion of a diatribe against miracles by the leader-writer in the Paris *Presse*: "If I was assured that a supernatural event of the most striking kind had taken place at this very time beside me on the Place de la Concorde, I would not turn aside in order to go and see it".

It was in this spirit of scientific "freethought" that another Parisian paper reported the day when Our Lady's demand was "Penance! Penance! Penance!": "This morning, the little comedian of the miller of Lourdes gathered an audience of about two thousand simple-minded souls around her at the Massabielle rock. The stupidity and mental cretinism of her followers is beyond belief. The little *voyante* treats them like a band of monkeys, getting them to perform all sorts of mummeries . . ."

Nor is there any reason to suppose that this particular kind of diabolic activity, comparatively pedestrian though it is, will ever cease to attack Lourdes.

III

The Time

THE meaning of Lourdes in relation to its time is more immediately apparent to the French than to the English. A Frenchman takes the historical background of his country for granted, with the consequence that the mere placing of a date or name has for him overtones and implications which, for the English reader, are completely lacking. It is not so much that these are lost in the translation of French lives of Bernadette as that they are not there to translate. A chapter such as this, for instance, would be an insistence on the obvious. But an English reader, unless he be a specialist in modern European history, cannot be presumed to have a knowledge of nineteenth-century French politics. And, without it, the significance of the time of Our Lady's appearances is largely lost.

(I)

France, during the last half of the nineteenth century, was the scene of a specific struggle for the Faith. If the triumph of atheism in the French Revolution had been checked in action by Napoleon I's Concordat, the memories of the anti-religious party were long and their hopes of eventual triumph undiminished. The court of Napoleon III was riddled with scepticism and, for political reasons, if for no other, the Emperor was inclined towards the Liberals. By about 1862 (the year when the Bishop of Tarbes had finished his examination of the evidence concerning the Grotto and issued his pastoral permitting belief in the authenticity of the Apparitions), the Catholic journal, *L'Univers*, had been suppressed: the Society of St Vincent de Paul had been dissolved; Renan, a bitter opponent of Christianity, had been by Imperial decree appointed to the Chair of Hebrew at the Collège de France; and, also by Imperial decree, a Marshal of France had been appointed as Grand Master of the Grand Orient Masons, who formed the secret and militant core of the anti-Catholic attack.

The judgment of the Bishop of Tarbes acted as an immediate challenge, which was taken up at once by the secular Press. *Le Siècle*, *Le Constitutionel* and *Le Pays* thundered into action—"a vast conspiracy obviously organized by the clerical party against any advance of the human spirit" . . . "They desire to keep our people in the swaddling clothes of ridiculous superstitions" . . . "a system of spiritual debasement" . . . "Lourdes is only a very small detail indeed in a whole neo-Catholic undertaking that can only be regarded as deplorable."

The Catholics, too, were not slow to respond. From all parts of France came offerings and professions of faith. A wave of hope welled up. In the four years that followed, from 1862 to 1866, Bernadette's active apostolate at Lourdes, when at interviews she convinced incessant visitors, checked something of the effect of the atheist propaganda, and in 1867, the year after she retired to Nevers, the opening of the railway to Lourdes ensured ever-increasing numbers of pilgrims who had come to see for themselves. On the eve of the Franco-Prussian war, Lourdes had been made safe, at least for France.

As B. G. Sandhurst has put it in *We Saw Her*, epitomizing this stage in the story: "In 1870 the Third Republic came to power. The persecution began. Religious teaching was forbidden in schools, the monks and nuns were expelled, Catholics were penalized by loss of positions. *The new shrine was untouched*. The Grand Orient Masons would have liked to have got their claws into it, if they had dared, but it was too late".

(II)

1870 was, indeed, a year of destiny for France. The military defeat at the hands of the Germans led to the Liberal-Republican triumph and the intensification of the assault on the Church, while the Vatican Council definition *de fide* of Papal Infallibility led to the defection, within the Church, of those "liberal" Catholics who had, albeit unconsciously, absorbed too much of the spirit of the secular age.

Bernadette herself summed it up in her simple way, though her utterances had no direct reference to it.

In the autumn of 1870, in the convent of Nevers, the Sisters were marvelling at a sky which "looked like a sea of blood", when Bernadette was heard to murmur: "And they are still unconverted!" She regarded the Prussians as merely "doing their job" as the instrument of punishment of France's sins; and when the Chevalier Cougenot des Mousseaux, concerned with "realism" came on a visit to her to enquire: "Have you had, either in the Grotto at Lourdes, or since, any revelations concerning the future and destiny of France?" Bernadette answered plainly: "No, sir".

"The Prussians are at the gates. Doesn't that make you afraid?"

"No, sir."

"So you think there is nothing to fear?"

"Yes, sir."

"What?"

" Bad Catholics."

"Nothing else? You fear nothing else?"

"No, sir."

Bernadette's mission was entirely spiritual, though Sister Catherine Labouré, who was still alive, could have reminded the Chevalier of a prophecy which, forty years earlier, Our Lady had made to her, in the first of the apparitions connected with the Miraculous Medal: "The Archbishop will die and the streets of Paris will run with blood". With the rising of the Commune in the May of 1871, this was fulfilled. Among the atrocities perpetrated by the temporarily victorious Commune during the "Bloody Week" was the massacre of many priests, including the Archbishop of Paris.

As if in reparation there was held, three weeks later, the first of twenty-four pilgrimages to the Grotto. "Whole provinces began to move towards Massabielle."

In counter-attack Dr. Voison of the Salpêtrière provided a much-publicized declaration: "The miracle at Lourdes rests on the conviction of a child subject to hallucinations who is now confined in the Convent of the Ursulines at Nevers".

The Bishop of Nevers issued, through the Press, an immediate reply: "I have the honour to inform you

(1)   that Sister Marie-Bernard has never set foot in the Convent of the Ursulines at Nevers;

(2)   that while it is true that she lives at Nevers in the Convent of the Sisters of Charity and Christian Instruction, she entered the Convent and she remains there perfectly at her own free will;

(3)   that, far from being subject to hallucinations, she is exceptionally well-balanced and serene.

Further, I freely invite the illustrious professor to come and verify in person the accuracy of the above declaration . . . I will undertake to put him in touch with Sister Marie-Bernard immediately and in order that there shall be no doubt as to her identity, I will ask the Chief Imperial Prosecutor to be good enough to present her to him. He will then be allowed to look at her, to question her, even to weary her, for as long as he likes . . ."

In spite of the fact that the Bishop also offered to pay the doctor's expenses, the famous scientist neither replied nor went.

The anti-Christian mobs, however, continued an attack, effective enough with its limits. Sacred banners were burnt and pilgrims abused on the streets. Yet the crowds going to Lourdes grew. "Several thousands of people at a time would shout: 'Long live the Immaculate Conception' as though it were a war-cry" and in 1872 there was a national "pilgrimage of expiation", in which every Department of France was represented by its appropriate banner. Known as "the Pilgrimage of Banners", it included, among its 50,000 people, twenty-four bishops, 110 deputies, forty senators and several generals and high officials.

Alarmed, the opposition consolidated itself by an unparalleled pronouncement. The Freemasons, however anti-Catholic, were theoretically Deists and imposed on their members a belief in God under the title of "the Great Architect", but in 1873 the Grand Master waived this obligation in order to admit atheist scientists who, in the name of "education" and "intellectual emancipation" could be of service in the attack on the Church.

On both sides, during the 'seventies, the struggle was recognized for what it was. The Catholics proclaimed "Between the Church and the Revolution there exists absolute incompatibility" and rallied to the cry—*Gesta Dei per Francos.* Gambetta, soon to be in power and able to start the persecution, replied with: "Clericalism is the enemy".

In Lourdes, at the beginning of July, 1876, the "chapel" for which Our Lady had asked—the basilica of the Immaculate Conception—was consecrated by the Archbishop of Paris and the statue of Our Lady of Lourdes crowned by the Apostolic Nuncio. To this ceremony came a hundred thousand of the faithful of ten nations. Lourdes was established as a place of international pilgrimage. In less than a year, the forces dedicated to the destruction of the Faith in France, led by Gambetta, won power at the elections. But it was just too late. Again Lourdes was safe, this time not only for France but for the world.

The part played by Lourdes in the history of these years is recognized even in the sober, critical pages of the *Cambridge Modern History.* There one may read the lament that in view of "the increase of pilgrimages to Lourdes and Rome and the cult of relics, it might have seemed that the times of the Restoration had returned" and that "innumerable pilgrimages reached Paray-le-Monial and Lourdes, to the chant of 'Save Rome and France', France seemed wholly won over to the Holy See, as the champion of Christ and Rome dreamed of by ardent Catholics".

And through the darker days of the 'eighties and 'nineties, with the expulsion of the Jesuits, the compulsory secularization of schools, the new laws on divorce, the wave of pro-Semitism consequent on the Dreyfus case* and the break with the Vatican, Lourdes continued to bear its unique witness. In 1883, the twenty-fifth anniversary of the Visions, the crowds were larger than ever and, as Michel de Saint-Pierre says in *Bernadette and Lourdes,* "a veritable

---

* Zola, whose spirited defence of Dreyfus is always remembered, made also a violent attack on Bernadette.

human sea beat against the walls of the Grotto, already blackened by the smoke of holy candles and festooned with abandoned crutches".

. (III)

"Though you will not believe me", Jesus once said to the unbelieving Jews, "believe the works"; and again, in His discourse to the disciples on the eve of His Passion, He repeated the admonition that, should doubt assail them, they were to "believe for the very works' sake". On another, earlier, occasion, "He began to upbraid the cities wherein were done the most of His miracles, for that they had not done penance: 'Woe to thee, Corozain, woe to thee, Bethsaida: for if in Tyre and Sidon had been wrought the miracles that have been wrought in you, they had long ago done penance in sackcloth and ashes' ".

"The miracles wrought by our Lord Jesus Christ", says St Augustine, "are indeed divine works and admonitions of God to the human mind that it should rise to the understanding of Him by the things that are seen . . . In His mercy, He hath reserved to Himself certain works, which He should do at suitable times, beside the usual course and order of nature that, so, they in whose regard His daily works have become cheap, might be amazed at the sight of works, not indeed greater but unusual."

Our Lord's miracles were thus "signs" pointing beyond themselves, to the ultimate truths about the nature of God and His universe, to His own Person, to man's need of redemption through Him. They were "signs" that could be understood by anyone. Ultimately they admitted of but one interpretation and men neglected it at their eternal peril. "And thou, Capharnaum, thou shalt go down even unto

D

hell. For if in Sodom had been wrought the miracles that
had been wrought in thee, perhaps it had remained unto
this day. But I say unto you that it shall be more tolerable
for the land of Sodom in the day of judgment than for
thee."

The miracles at Lourdes must equally be understood in
this way. Our Lady never mentioned miracles or promised
that anyone would be cured there. Bernadette herself, as
far as can be ascertained, never admitted more than that she
had heard of cures taking place. The reiterated message was
"Penance! Penance! Penance!" In Father Martindale's
words: "We may be very grateful for the miracles at
Lourdes, but will not forget to treat them, as the Jews
were meant to treat our Lord's, as 'signs' pointing further
than themselves. Even so, Lourdes is not primarily an
instrument for 'proving' the supernatural to those who do
not believe it: it exists primarily for our own sanctification".

The miracles performed for a hundred years at Lourdes
are, therefore, in one sense—and, perhaps, primarily—an
act of divine charity to unbelievers, giving them notice, in
objective and verifiable terms they can understand, of the
obligation of conversion. "Scientific progress", " Freethought", "Liberal humanism" and all other varieties of
intellectual agnosticism could ignore the spiritual message
of Bernadette but they could not ignore—and remain
honest—the philosophical and theological implications of
the cures. (The frank atheists, of course, could not and
cannot, *ex hypothesi*, admit the existence of miracles and so
were, and are, precluded by irrational prejudice from any
attempt at investigation.)

Catholics, who are not by faith bound to admit any
miracles except those recorded in Holy Writ, were the first
to demand the most stringent tests before they gave their

intellectual assent to the authenticity of the cures. The conditions demanded by the Church were that the sickness really existed (this is to exclude not only neurotic cases but those incompletely diagnosed); that the malady in question must be dangerous or difficult, if not impossible to cure; that the illness must not have arrived at the stage at which it could develop with equal facility towards a cure or towards death . If remedies had previously been applied, in the ordinary way of treatment, there must be absolute certainty that they have nothing to do with the cure, which must be unexpected, instantaneous, perfect, and complete, and must take place in direct relation to some religious act on the part of the sick person (prayer, pilgrimage, bathing with the Massabielle water, etc.) or on the part of other persons (prayer, blessing, etc.).

The Lourdes miracles have already a literature of their own, establishing their reality beyond any doubt; and as early as 1906 a visit was made by 346 medical men of various nationalities and different creeds who published the following declaration: "The cures obtained at Lourdes are brought about by a specific factor which cannot be rationally explained as the result of natural forces alone". Today, according to Dr Leuret, the President of the Medical Office, "both doctors and theologians have on the whole a tendency to try to prove that there has been no 'miracle' rather than to discover exactly what has happened". Which is as it should be. No test can be too stringent.

But still, unfortunately, the bad faith of certain "specialists" persists. To quote Dr Leuret again: "There are medical men who, believing that a miracle is 'something that cannot happen', refuse to examine the facts, or even confirm what they have previously stated, or allow access to documents which might provide arguments against their convictions. I remember the case of a patient suffering from

plastic peritonitis. An operation detached the main adher-
ences. A relapse was radiologically established. The
surgeon decided that his intervention could be postponed
seeing that the patient was in a position to take liquid food.
The patient then made a pilgrimage to Lourdes where a
cure was obtained and radiologically confirmed. The
radiologist then refused to allow either the patient or his
doctor to have access to the radiological records prior to
the cure, even declaring that he had not seen the patient
before his departure for Lourdes".

If this is possible today—Dr Leuret's book was published
in 1950—it may be imagined how prevalent was the same
attitude in the France of the years we have been discussing.
It made its first appearance in Lourdes itself at the time of
the Visions and the first cures.

The Mayor, M. Anselme Lacadé, in an endeavour to
prove that the spring water contained mineral healing
properties, had a special analysis made by an obliging
scientist, M. Latour of Trie. If mineral properties could be
proved, the spring would become a property of the town
and religious processions to the Grotto could, quite
lawfully, be forbidden. Also, the sick could be charged for
their cures and Lourdes might gain fame and profit as a
spa.

M. Latour, having made his examination, declared that
the water contained large elements of "chloride, silicate,
carbonate, iron oxide and sodium sulphate". M. Lacadé,
delighted, paid him sixty francs for this convenient pronouncement. Certain town councillors, however, were
suspicious and insisted on a second opinion from an
acknowledged expert.

This analysis, by M. Filhol, Professor in the Faculty of
Science at Toulouse, exposed the falsehood and showed
beyond all contradiction that the water was in plain

language "drinkable water, containing the same elements as most spring water".*

In 1875—that is to say, at a critical point in the struggle for the soul of nineteenth-century France and not long after the scientists had been enlisted by the Grand Orient—one of the most spectacular cures, an inescapable "sign", was wrought by the intercession of Our Lady. The fact that it occurred, not at Lourdes itself, but at a Belgian grotto dedicated to Our Lady of Lourdes, made it the more remarkable.

Eight years earlier, M. de Rudder had been injured by a falling tree. He had neglected the injury and, when examined on April 7, 1875, he was found to be suffering from "a compound suppurating fracture of the upper third of the tibia and fibula of the left leg". While he was praying at the Belgian grotto, the fracture "was instantly consolidated, the wound closed and the bones solidly reconstituted". It was an instantaneous cure in defiance of all known laws: and de Rudder's fellow townsmen who, the previous evening, had helped him aboard the train could hardly believe their eyes when they saw him return "walking, running and jumping".

* There have been many subsequent analyses, all of which have confirmed the conclusion that the water of the well is pure and simple; common drinkable water. Secular, non-Catholic laboratories have established that "the water of the well is ice-cold, yet no sick person contracts pneumonia and no healthy person has become ill after sudden immersion in it. The water should be full of bacteria of the most atrocious diseases, contaminated by the thousands of sick who come to Lourdes. Nevertheless, the water does not infect anyone; when samples of the well were analysed after the immersion of hundreds of sick the water showed no signs of containing bacteria". Another analysis of the well for the purpose of ascertaining its mineralogical composition found that it had no therapeutic value. "It is not radioactive, antibiotic or antiseptic. It is simply a pure, potable water."

The Medical Bureau expresses no opinion on any healing before the end of the second year after the patient has claimed a cure. Its purpose is merely to establish the facts of the case. There are always between fifteen and seventy members present at each discussion and they include non-Catholics and anti-Catholics. Between eight hundred and fifteen hundred physicians, from most of the countries of the world, take part annually in the discussions. "In 1952 there were 41 university professors, 121 hospital directors, 97 surgeons, 64 pediatricians, 63 specialists on tuberculosis, 54 gynæcologists, 30 ophthamologists, 20 heart specialists and 604 general practitioners. Numerically the different nationalities were represented as follows: 734 French, 229 Italians, 157 Belgians, 47 British, 25 Germans, 26 Swiss, 21 Americans, 15 Africans, eight Indians and one Syrian."

After his death, a post-mortem was made. Dr Lafitte, the authority on osteo-arthritis, has pronounced: "Everything had taken place as though a good practitioner anxious to restore the solidity and the plane of the bone without any shortening—the first important point—had reduced the fracture, carefully matching the bones, and then consolidated the joint. But all that work, which would normally require several weeks, if not months, was performed in an instant. This is something which upsets all our acquired notions of osseous pathology. It is the unmistakable sign that there was intervention by a power which we can neither know nor check. In other words, a miracle. The hand of God was present".

When the forces of atheism were politically triumphant in France and the religious orders were expelled in 1880, the Georgian Fathers, driven from their house at Montauban, returned to Constantinople. Here, on the Feast of the Annunciation, March 25, 1881, they dedicated an altar to Our Lady of Lourdes in their chapel, set up a statue which was a replica of the one in the Grotto and had spring water sent them. The cures were so many and so immediate that the Archbishop of Sardis had to set up a commission to enquire into them. A Jew of Orta-Keui, who was deaf in both ears, and a child of thirteen club-footed from birth were instantaneously cured. There was, too, an anticipation of one of the most famous cures at Lourdes itself (the so-called "needle cure" of 1886*). In 1882 an Armenian woman came to the Georgians' chapel with a fragment of needle in her finger. The surgeons had given up hope of getting rid of it: inflammation extended from her hand to her arm and

* Celestine Dubois had a piece of broken needle in her hand for seven years. The hand became swollen and the fingers contracted and bent. Incisions were made and the wound was kept open for three weeks, but they could not get the bit of needle out. On August 20th, 1886, she thrust her hand into one of the piscinas at Lourdes and the needle, forcing its way through a passage more than three inches long, came out all of itself after suddenly passing beneath the skin at the top of the thumb.

her suffering was very great. The woman made a novena before the altar of Our Lady of Lourdes, at the end of which the needle came out of its own accord and the inflammation subsided.

The fame of these happenings was considerable. Besides Catholics, Greeks, Armenians and Bulgarian schismatics, Turkish officers and soldiers, pashas and dervishes and Jewish merchants mingled in the crowds that came to the convent. And Mohammedans and Jews were cured as well as Christians.

Yet still scepticism continued. In 1903, the great scientist who was to become a Nobel Prize physicist and Medical Director of the Rockerfeller Institute, Dr Alexis Carrell, a sceptic of sceptics, visited Lourdes and was converted to a belief in the miracles by what he saw and tested. Among his literary remains, he left an account of his visit, which was published in 1949. In it he noted: "My colleagues persist in obstinate silence and unpardonable indifference" and added this judgment, which is as true today as it was at the beginning of the century: "Their [doctors'] professional studies have caused them to touch on many scientific problems, but most of them have never done any real scientific work and have not the slightest idea of what experimental research really involves ... The lack of any definite method and the intellectual mediocrity of many of them make them incapable of honest criticism. Most of them still believe that there is nothing but trickery at Lourdes. *But they dare not test their belief*".

But the fact remains that between 1858 and the outbreak of the 1914 war there were at least 1,600 miracles, whose authenticity cannot be denied; and that between 1914 and 1955 the Medical Bureau attested and the ecclesiastical authorities approved a further 262. And, whatever their full significance, one must surely agree with Fr Agostino

Gemelli, O.F.M., writing in 1956 on *The Lesson of Lourdes*: "In this our time, so pagan, rationalistic and blasphemous, in which the most diverse ideologies and social systems have made use of subtle and all-pervading means to rob men of the patrimony of the Faith, God, through Lourdes, has wished to demonstrate that He is our Lord and Creator who controls the forces of nature".

And when it is remembered that those "diverse ideologies and social systems" are, for the most part, the consequences of the Revolution in France, spreading from there to America on one side of the world and to Germany and Russia on the other, the significance of the time of the Visions becomes inescapable.

IV

The Person

A<small>T</small> the time of Our Lady's first appearance to her, Bernadette had just passed her fourteenth birthday. Her family, in the direst poverty, was living in a one-roomed dungeon in a slum in Lourdes. She had returned to them a fortnight earlier from an eight-months' stay at her foster-mother's farm, four miles away, where for some of the time she had tended the sheep. She was small for her age, looking not more than twelve. She was asthmatic—a permanent legacy of the cholera which had nearly killed her during an epidemic when she was eleven.

These facts, however, do not justify the legend that she was a miserably poor and not very strong little shepherdess, a simple peasant, with no experience of life. That conception is based on the "fallacy of the moment", the outlook which confines itself to a static picture based on the "accidents" of a dramatic-moment-in-time, and makes no allowance for continuous experience and development implicit in that moment—as if, to use a popular analogy, a "still" of the final scene were the same thing as a showing of the whole film.

Even the conventional associations of certain words are misleading. A French *paysan* is by no means the equivalent of an English "peasant", and a Pyrenean *paysan* is practically untranslatable. Neither does "a girl of fourteen" as that entity exists in English civilization today call up the mental image of a girl of the same age in the extreme south of

France a hundred years ago. Bernadette's mother, for
instance, was only seventeen when she was married and
hardly eighteen when Bernadette was born. Moreover, at
fourteen, Bernadette had lived nearly half her span of years;
in it she had experienced many vicissitudes and had seen
life from many angles. She had known freedom and
happiness as well as servitude and responsibility. She had
been an almost "spoilt" child of a property-owning and
somewhat irresponsible family before she was involved in a
poverty so grinding that her younger brother ate candle
grease from church candles to assuage his hunger, and in the
social disgrace of seeing her father indicted as a thief.

She was "only fourteen"—whatever that may be held to
involve in emotion and experience—but does one ever feel
so keenly or see so clearly as in childhood? Bernadette, like
all the saints, was thoroughly prepared for her mission.

(1)

Sheltered by the rock of the Castle, on the bank of the
Lapaca, a strong stream flowing into the river Gave, stood
the Boly mill. This was held on lease by the Casterot family,
millers of some substance in the town. When the head of
the family died, comparatively young, his widow arranged a
marriage between her younger daughter, the seventeen-
year-old Louise, and a journeyman miller of Lourdes,
François Soubirous, eighteen years her senior. He was "a
simple man of gentle manners and a shy disposition" who
had been engaged in the past to help at the mill. But,
however good he may have been as an assistant, he had not
the temperament for management which his mother-in-law
had hoped for when she made the match; nor did the young

wife, gay, irresponsible and openhanded, provide a counter-balance to his unsuitability as a principal in a highly-competitive trade. Payment of bills was not insisted on, and even when it was made the debtors often consumed in hospitality more than they paid in settlement. Also, out of the charity of his heart, François Soubirous constantly agreed to grind corn for poor people for the love of God. Which is not a way to make money. Ten years after Berna-dette's birth all M. Casterot's savings were spent and the Soubirous could no longer afford to pay the rent.

The decline was, of course, gradual and Bernadette's early childhood lacked neither security nor a relative affluence. In addition to her family and a generous supply of aunts, there was one friend of her mother who was de-voted to her, Marie Lagües, the wife of a farmer at Bartrès.

When Bernadette was six months old, her mother, who was expecting another child, was burnt by a candle falling on her dress and was unable to continue feeding Bernadette. As it happened, Marie Lagües had just lost her first child and Bernadette was taken to Bartrès for suckling and weaning. Though she was returned to her mother five months later (on the death of Louise Soubirous' second child), Marie Lagües had become deeply attached to her and thereafter when, on market days, she brought her farm produce to Lourdes "she would pass by the Soubirous house to give Bernadette a kiss and the child would be sure to find at the bottom of the big basket some cakes from Bartrès made specially for her". And throughout her childhood Berna-dette went to stay with her for a week in the spring and a week in the summer as special holidays.

When the Soubirous had to leave the Boly mill, Berna-dette, at ten, was under no illusions. When she had noticed the way things were going, she even asked her sixteen-year-old cousin to speak to her mother about her extravagant habits. And she was already responsible enough to be kept at home to help "manage" while her sister Toinette, two-and-a-half years younger, was sent to school at the Hospice.

Old Madame Casterot did what she could for the family and, when the crash came, rented for them another mill not far away—the Laborde mill. This, from the beginning, was disastrous. The equipment was poor; there was triumphant competition from the rich Lacadé mill, belonging to the family of the Mayor of Lourdes; and François Soubirous, as an acknowledged local "failure", was in no shape to retrieve the situation. For lack of orders, both he and his wife had to take what employment they could get. It was at this point that Bernadette had cholera.

Later that year—in October 1855—Grandmother Casterot died, leaving the Soubirous, as their share of her money, 900 francs. With this, François Soubirous rented another mill, a mile or two east of Lourdes, at Arcizac. The machinery of this mill was primitive, its product poor and the family had to live in a hut. When, during that severe winter, Bernadette's aunt-godmother (her mother's elder sister, Bernarde Nicolau) came to visit them, she heard the child coughing badly and took her back with her to her own house in Lourdes, to be warmer and better fed. In return for this hospitality, Bernadette helped to look after her young cousins and run the house.

Within six months, the Arcizac mill had failed even more completely than its predecessors and François Soubirous was reduced to working as a casual labourer in Lourdes at any job that he could get. He rented a "wretched hole" not far from the parish church, but, not being able to make ends meet, was turned out by the landlord and had to leave his only remaining good piece of furniture, a cupboard, in lieu of rent.

On All Saints' Day, 1856, the destitute family obtained

leave to live, for a nominal payment, in a room which had once been used as a local "dungeon" or nightly lock-up, but which had been abandoned as too insanitary even for the Lourdes "drunks". It was a stone room, about five yards square, with two small windows opening on to a tiny courtyard, in which there was a manure heap above the flagstones and a cess-pit below. Into this *cachot* the family moved their worldly possessions, which consisted of two beds, a box, two chairs and some red crockery. But there was also a rosary and a crucifix.

For seven months, Bernadette lived here with her father and mother, her eleven-year-old sister, Toinette, her six-year-old brother, Jean-Marie, and the baby, the eighteen-month-old Justin.* Her asthma became acute and in the June of 1857 she went back to her foster-mother at Bartrès, no longer as a "spoilt" visitor, but as a "help" to look after the children and the sheep in return for her board.

This same year her father was arrested on the charge of stealing two sacks of flour, and was kept in jail for a week. He was released for lack of evidence. In his defence, he explained that he had risen at three to bring some firewood back from Bartrès and admitted that he had taken a beam belonging to one of the Lourdes doctors.

At the end of January 1858—exactly a fortnight before the first appearance of Our Lady—Bernadette, of her own volition and on her own initiative, left Bartrès and returned to the *cachot*.

These were the outward circumstances which determined Bernadette's social status and human experience. Because of the one, she was, through no fault of her own, a natural "suspect"—an illiterate slum-dweller whose family was a by-word, whose father was known as a failure and believed

---

* Bernadette's youngest brother, Bernard, who lived till 1931, was not born till 1859,

to be a thief. Because of the other, she can have had few
illusions about the fickleness of circumstance or the
changeability of human nature. Even the affectionate
foster-mother at Bartrès, though she may have lost none of
her love, became at the end an employer with a family of
her own which, naturally, took first place. Deeply, even
passionately, as she loved her own mother, Bernadette had
no illusions about her. And the changing attitude of relatives,
neighbours and acquaintances as the family sank in the
social and economic scale could not have left her untouched.
To this was added illness which never allowed her to be
without some pain and which permanently prevented her
playing the boisterous games with other children which she
had delighted in.

It may be too much to say, as M. de Saint-Pierre does,
that on that day of Our Lady's first appearance to her
"Bernadette was perhaps the most wretched child in all
France"; but at least that judgment expresses what might
have been expected from the circumstances. Had the
circumstances, that is, represented the whole situation. One
ground indeed she had for sorrow. On the previous day the
bishop had visited Lourdes for a confirmation, but she had
not been among those who made their First Communion.

(ii)

In their years of prosperity, the Soubirous had sat
lightly to religion and Bernadette, growing up, watched
her parents gradually return to the practice of their faith as
the bad days came. In those impressionable years, it became
the oasis in the pitiless desert. On Sundays they never
missed Mass. They communicated at Easter and sometimes
oftener. Every night family prayers were said, and after the
prayer for the diocese, in *patois*, Bernadette led the Rosary,

concluding with the prayer of the Miraculous Medal, "O Mary, conceived without stain, pray for us who have recourse to thee". That was all she knew of the Faith—the *Our Father*, the *Hail Mary*, the Creed and the "new" prayer. She could not read or write. She was not sent to school. No one taught her the catechism. Even her memory was bad. She was never, even to the end of her life, able to "meditate" in the formal sense of the term. But, at least from the age of eleven, she knew that the one thing above all others she wanted was Holy Communion—which, in those days, before the reform of St Pius X, meant that she must first know her catechism.

This was the characteristic mark of her childhood. She would accept everything—hunger, pain, overwork, denial of the schooling which even her younger sister had, poverty, contempt, occasional ill-treatment and a responsibility which was a burden for her years—with a resignation and sweetness of disposition themselves almost a miracle. But this she would not accept. Other things might be, as she said, God's wish. This deprivation of the Blessed Sacrament most palpably was not. On this issue, and on this alone, she was prepared to fight.

How persistently she asked her parents, we do not know; but we do know that her mother was conscience-stricken at last when, on Corpus Christi, 1857, she saw Bernadette crying uncontrollably in church as other children went up to make their First Communion. She was allowed to go, almost immediately afterwards, to Bartrès not only for her health's sake, but because her foster-mother, who had been told of this, gave the assurance that she would be able to go to catechism there more easily than at Lourdes.

When she arrived at Bartrès, she was immediately enrolled in the catechism class held every Sunday and twice during the week. The schoolmaster, who occasionally took the class in the priest's absence, reported: "She finds it difficult to learn by heart, as she cannot read; but she takes great pains to understand the inner meaning of the explanations that are given her. She is also very attentive and, above all, very devout and unassuming". But within four months the parish priest had left to enter a Benedictine monastery and, as his successor was some time in coming, the lessons ceased.

Her foster-mother did what she could to make up for it; but there were only the tired evenings of a hard-worked day. "Mistress used to teach her a little in the evenings", the maid reported, "but poor Bernadette was very hard to teach. She had to repeat the same word three or four times and then she forgot it, so much so that her foster-mother used to throw down the book in despair saying: 'You'll never learn anything'."*

Bernadette, too, realized that she would never learn anything that way. Holy Communion seemed as far off as ever. Within two months, she had made up her mind. One day when she was looking after the sheep, she saw a woman of Lourdes passing and said to her: "Please tell my parents I want to come home to Lourdes and join a class to prepare for my First Communion. Ask them to come and fetch me".

The woman did as she was asked, but Louise Soubirous took no notice of the message. As she did not come, Bernadette then asked M. Lagües for permission to visit her parents. He agreed, but told her to be back the next day.

Bernadette, arriving unexpectedly at the *cachot*, announced: "I've come back to go to catechism" and stayed there for three days until arrangements were at last made for her to receive instruction at the Hospice so that she might make her First Communion at Corpus Christi.

---

* In justice to Bernadette, it must be remembered that she was learning the catechism in French, which to her was virtually a foreign language that she did not learn to speak even tolerably till she was seventeen: and that she had never, till this autumn, had any discipline of learning.

Then she returned to Bartrès to explain and to say good-bye. Asked why she was so late, she answered: "I must go home. M. le Curé is going to prepare children for First Communion and if I am in Lourdes I can join the class". She left the following day.

Much has been written, speculatively, of Bernadette's stay at Bartrès; of the spiritual idyll of a shepherdess meditating in the fields on the wonders of Heaven and earth and being led, mysteriously and intuitively, back to Lourdes, not knowing why but arriving there in time for Our Lady's rendezvous at the Grotto. It may be true, though it does not fit what we know of Bernadette or the recorded facts; and it seems rather part of that pious legend which told of little miracles worked during those months— a legend which Bernadette herself impatiently demolished with: "There is not a word of truth in it".

The real Bernadette wanted intensely and single-mindedly one thing—the necessary preparation for receiving the Body and Blood of Jesus Christ. For this, because she could not get it at Lourdes, she went to Bartrès; and when she found she could not get it at Bartrès she came back to Lourdes and insisted on it. She took her place at the bottom of a catechism class with children half her age. She had been only twice and still knew nothing but the Rosary when one cold afternoon she went to Massabielle to gather dead wood for a fire and met Christ's Mother with her rosary on her arm.

(III)

Bernadette had seen Our Lady seventeen times—the last meeting was still in the future—before she made, at last, her First Communion on Corpus Christi, 1858. She understood,

E

though she was still unable to memorize her catechism. To the question: "Bernadette Soubirous, what do you know?" she had answered: "The *Our Father*, the *Hail Mary* and the *I believe in God*", to be told: "Then you know enough to say your Rosary". She had answered two other questions satisfactorily. During the retreat, "her demeanour, her composure and her attentiveness left nothing to be desired", according to the report the parish priest made to the bishop. When she made her Communion "she seemed entirely absorbed in the sacred action in which she was engaged". Some people wondered whether she would experience an ecstasy, such as she had at the Grotto. "But nothing happened. Bernadette went up to the altar with her hands joined, received God and came back to her place without giving any sign but that of a deep and boundless happiness", wrote one who was present.

Afterwards, when she was asked: "Which gave you the greatest pleasure: to receive the Body of Christ or to speak with the Blessed Virgin?" she answered:

"I don't know which gave me the most pleasure. The two things go together and they can't be compared. All I know is that I was very happy both times".

And the theological exactness of the answer was, it may be, revealed to her in its fullness when, on the Feast of Our Lady of Carmel, she made her Communion—it was her fourth—and, a few hours later, was summoned by that "compulsion of the heart" to the meadow from which she saw Mary in the barricaded and deserted Grotto for the last time. We know that Our Lady had never looked more lovely and that her presence obliterated the barrier and the distance. She spoke no word. "She simply let her child gaze her fill, leaving her consoled, happy and ready to face the long night of separation and suffering that lay ahead." But through that long night, the Blessed Sacrament was there.

The inter-relation continued throughout Bernadette's life—she was to speak again in a letter written on Corpus Christi just before she went to Nevers, of the "great happiness" which she experienced when she received Holy Communion in the Grotto itself—and it has continued in Lourdes itself. "The City of Mary" is also, as St Pius X named it, "the City of the Eucharist."

In 1880, the year after Bernadette's death, there was instituted at Lourdes that procession of the Blessed Sacrament among the sick assembled on the Esplanade of the Rosary which recalls the scenes of the New Testament when Christ in His Incarnate Body moved among the halt and the deaf and the blind and the sick of many diseases. It is a scene which has often been described and yet remains indescribable—the moment when the Sacramental Body in the monstrance is raised high in blessing over the great crowd, prostrate in adoration. The simplicity of a sentence by Mgr Trochu is, perhaps, best: "Every afternoon, between five and six o'clock, it is Corpus Christi in Lourdes".

The implications are infinite; but at least among them there should be room for the memory of the determined little girl tramping back from Bartrès in search of the Blessed Sacrament, to discover that Our Lady herself, who knew the intensity of her desire, had condescended to fill the interim.

(IV)

Bernadette's human personality thus emerges clearly enough. At fourteen she had to a notable degree three kinds of courage—the passive courage which can uncomplainingly accept outward circumstances combined with the active courage which is prepared to fight relentlessly for its

spiritual rights and needs, and the physical fortitude which
can endure pain and weakness.

Her experience of life had given her a shrewdness of
assessment which, in a nature less spiritual, might well have
become cynicism. Even her lack of "education" was, in a
sense, an advantage in that it meant that the clarity of her
native perceptions was not befogged by the pretentiousness
of semi-literacy. Having nothing to unlearn, she could
accept, without hesitation, the simplicity of the supernatural.

If she was not disturbed by the cross-questioning of
police, magistrates, doctors and sceptics, that may be, at
least in part, that she had no reason to be. They could not
hurt her more than life had already hurt her. Even the
prison, with which they threatened her, could not be much
worse confinement than the *cachot*; and her kindly father had
already endured it. That she had any undue respect for the
representatives of authority is to the last degree unlikely.
Those biographers who suppose that she was "awed" by
the policeman, Jacomet, the prosecutor, Dutour, or even
the Mayor, Lacadé, reveal by that judgment little but their
own complacent social assumptions. Jacomet and Dutour
(who was an unpleasant man by any standards) were
merely the men who had arrested and prosecuted her father
after the competition from the Lacadé mill had finally
ruined him. She had every excuse for disliking them—
though there is no evidence that her charity, except on one
occasion, failed—but she had none for respecting them,
especially since their object was not to establish the truth
of the circumstances but merely to make her appear a liar.

Her passage-at-arms with Jacomet, who altered her
statement in order to trap her, is, if anything, slightly *de
haut en bas*.

"So the lady was about nineteen years old?"

"No, sir. I said, sixteen or seventeen years old."

"Oh, perhaps you did. Now, this lady was dressed in a blue robe with a white sash—."

"No, sir. You've put down that wrong: I said a white robe with a blue sash."

"Did you? But this story of yours is pure invention. You've learnt it by heart."

"I don't understand."

"Who put you up to saying that the Virgin has appeared at Massabielle?"

"No one, sir."

"Have it your own way, but now you're going to promise me you won't go back to that grotto any more."

"No, sir. I can't promise you that because I have promised the Lady I will."

"Then I shall have you put in prison."

Bernadette, unimpressed by the threat, did not answer.

Later, she was taken before Dutour, and she has left us her own account of the interview: "I told him everything and he wrote it down. At the end of it he read out what he had written, but it was just the same as with the Commissioner of Police. I mean he read out some things I had not said. So I said: 'I didn't say that to you, sir'. But he said I had said it and I said I had not. However, in the end and after we had argued about it, he admitted he had made a mistake. Then he went on reading aloud, making new mistakes all the time and telling me he had what the commissioner (Jacomet) had put down and that what I was saying now was quite different. I told him that what I was saying to him was exactly what I had said to the commissioner and that if the commissioner had made mistakes, it was not my fault. Then he told his wife to send for the commissioner and a gendarme to take me to prison for the night. By this time my poor mother was crying and she kept looking at me and when she heard we were to be put in prison she cried all the more. But I consoled her by saying: 'Going to prison shouldn't make you cry; we haven't done any harm to anyone'. Then he offered us seats before going away to wait for the reply. My mother took a chair because she was shaking all over, after having stood there for two hours".

But Bernadette did not take a chair. For once she allowed herself the luxury of a devastating retort.

"No", she said, "I might dirty it"; and sat, cross-legged and unperturbed, on the floor.*

Bernadette's examinations by the civil authorities and the scientists they called to their aid when they wanted to put her in an asylum are of no value except in estimating her character (and, incidentally, their own). For one thing, we now know that the official records are, in Canon Belleney's words, full of "numerous, flagrant and indisputable errors". For another—and more importantly—by their *a priori* assumptions, the secular authorities were bound not to admit what had in fact taken place. For them, miracles did not happen; so that it would be as foolish to rely on their testimony as to accept a colour-blind man's description of a rainbow.

The only competent judges were representatives of the Church. The Appearances might be, as they said, "a miracle, imagination or deceit". Like the secular authorities, they were inclined to believe it was not the first; even more stringently than the secular authorities they were bound to leave no loophole for doubt and to proceed on the other hypotheses; but they could not exclude the possibility that it might be a miracle after all.

* Bernadette was later so distressed by the memory of her bitterness that, twenty years after the episode, she recalled it with tears in her eyes and the comment: "How wicked I was!" Nevertheless, as M. de Saint-Pierre has remarked, "for those of us who aren't saints there is something very satisfying about it;" and it at least illustrates her refusal to be either impressed or intimidated by the authorities.

Thus, while the official investigations reveal Bernadette's character, the ecclesiastical questioning—and that alone—is relevant to the authenticity of her message. The testing was at the hands of the parish priest of whom, unlike the police and the magistrates, she was a little afraid.

NOTE

JACOMET'S accounts of his interviews with Bernadette on February 21 and March 18, the drafts of his reports to the Prefect and many other documents which had been presumed lost (and are noted as "not recovered" in the 1957 English translation of Francis Trochu's *Saint Bernadette Soubirous*) have now been made available and were published in full in the first volume of René Laurentin's definitive *Lourdes : Dossier des documents authentiques*, in Paris in December 1957.

There is in them one passage above all which seems to me to establish Jacomet's bad faith. As a postscript to his draft of the first interview with Bernadette on February 21, he writes : " We thought it right to give some words of advice to this child ; we asked her to promise to stop her visits to the Grotto ; we told her that what she thought she saw was only the effect of hallucination and that it was in the interest of her [an illegible word : ? vertu : ? santé] to give up all these visions. ' All right ! I promise you not to go to the Grotto again : but ', she said to me *crying copiously, I ask you one favour. Papa and Mamma take the opposite view ; you must forbid them to force me to go to the Grotto. It tires me. I don't want to go there.*' "

The calligraphy of the passage in italics, though indubitably Jacomet's, is twice as large as the rest and is written with another pen and another (blacker) ink. The writing shows signs of considerable agitation. (Was this the moment, when, according to Bernadette, his hand was shaking so much "that he couldn't find the hole in the inkwell"?)

This is so completely contrary to all the facts established by every other eyewitness and by the course of events that he did not include it in his first report to the Prefect on March 2; but I find myself unable to agree with l'Abbé Laurentin that "he had the honesty not to persist against the evidence". I should have thought it was merely shrewd self-preservation since the Prefect could, by that time, have easily ascertained that he was officially lying.

V

Bernadette and the Parish Priest

MARIE-DOMINIQUE PEYRAMALE, the parish priest and Rural Dean of Lourdes, was the son of a doctor. With his wide reading, his intellectual liveliness and his social certainty, he could, as one biographer has expressed it, "hold his own in any conversation with the most cultured men of the town". Though these qualities are, in one sense, the least important thing about him—for he was first and foremost, as was fitting, an intrepid shepherd of souls—they are sufficiently relevant to the story of Bernadette to merit an initial emphasis. Even if he had held no position in Lourdes, he would still have been one of the few men in the town whose considered opinion on events would have been worth having. When, finally convinced by Bernadette, he became her champion, he was able to deal with doctors and lawyers on their own ground. And the Bishop of Tarbes, who was a peasant, deferred to his judgment from first to last.

(I)

In the year 1858, he had been in Lourdes for four years. He was just 47. Tall and broad, of the mountaineer type, he was tireless in the service of his parishioners and "with his patched and mended cassock, his well-worn boots and his battered shovel hat" he was one of the best-known figures of the town. The Lourdais, whatever their religious convictions, had a healthy respect for one who, with nothing but his walking stick, had one evening kept at bay and cowed three wolves from the mountain-side; and, on another plane, they knew that his purse was always open to the poor.

They were a little afraid of him. He did not suffer fools gladly. His speech was short and sharp and, when exasperated by stupidity, he was known to thunder at the top of his powerful voice. But his deep piety and his profound faith were universally recognized and to the faithful he was first, last and all the time a Father-in-God.

At the beginning of the events at the Grotto, he did not know Bernadette by sight, except for catching a glimpse of her in church. Her spiritual welfare was in the hands of two of the curates—Father Pène, who was in charge of the district where she lived, and Father Pomian, who was her confessor and the chaplain at the Hospice. Father Pène was, from the beginning, an enthusiastic believer in her and was prepared to argue the case with the Abbé Peyramale. Father Pomian tended to put the whole thing down to imagination until events forced him to change his mind; though even before he was convinced he gave Bernadette his permission to go to the Grotto in spite of the police prohibition, explaining to her that no one had any right to stop her. The third—and senior—curate, Father Serre, was an uncompromising opponent of Bernadette, and was suspected of reading and approving before publication the "attacking" articles in the local paper. Of the three, the Abbé Peyramale seems to have had most respect for the judgment, in this as in other matters, of Father Pomian.

On Saturday, February 13, Bernadette told Father Pomian in confession of the Lady's appearance to her the previous Thursday. Father Pomian said: "You must tell the parish priest about this".

"I'd rather you did, Father", said Bernadette.

"All right", agreed her confessor and, that evening, told the Abbé Peyramale of the circumstances. The parish priest dismissed it brusquely. "The pastor of a parish of four thousand souls", as Mgr Trochu has put it, "had other things to worry about. Lent was near and a Lent very much out of the ordinary. 1858 was a jubilee year: Pope Pius IX had ordered 'solemn public prayer that in all parts of the world good might triumph over evil'. M. Peyramale had to draw up a programme of special services and sermons: all much more important than the devotions of a schoolgirl in the deserted gully of Massabielle".

As it happened, as the Abbé was to discover, the event he dismissed was the answer to his preoccupation. A month later he was suggesting to the bishop that there was no need for special services, since "what has taken place at Lourdes has, rightly or wrongly, stirred the people so deeply that never have such large attendances been known at week day instructions".

(II)

On Friday, February 26, the day after the finding of the spring but before the significance of it (or, indeed, the nature of the water) had been realized, the Abbé Peyramale went over to Tarbes to make a report to the bishop. The matter had already reached a stage at which it was impossible to ignore it. That Friday, the police counted eight hundred spectators at the Grotto as Bernadette knelt in prayer. There were no clergy present, because the Abbé had forbidden them to go; but Father Pène's sister had been there regularly this first week of the 'Great Fortnight' and her reports to her brother had been passed on to the parish priest, accompanied by exhortations to go and see for himself.

"No," he replied, "if we go we shall certainly be accused of inspiring Bernadette and if the thing comes to nothing, the clergy will be ridiculed as fools and, what is more important, religion itself will suffer great harm. If God's hand is in it, then He has no need of us to accomplish His designs."

"God, if God is behind it," answered the curate, "will certainly triumph, but will it stand to our credit that we have not taken the trouble to find out and to make His presence known? And who can give the bishop the information he must have for forming a sound judgment unless we do?"

The Abbé Peyramale, though refusing to rescind the veto, agreed to consult the bishop before anything further happened. On his return from the interview, he told his staff: "I informed the bishop that there was a difference of opinion among us, some holding that we could attend the scenes taking place at the Grotto without impropriety: others believing that we should on no account do so. I asked him, point-blank: 'May we go, my Lord, or should we stand aloof?' After a few moments' thought he said: 'Go'. I objected: 'My Lord, if we go, it will be said that we are behind this girl and that it is because of our encouragement that she is playing these tricks'. 'Oh, in that case', said the bishop, 'don't go'."

Father Pène was not slow to point out that "the bishop's real decision was the first one and that the second was no more than an attempt to fall in with the parish priest's personal wishes and to leave the responsibility on his shoulders".

The Abbé's answer to this is unrecorded; but the veto remained.

Next day, Saturday, February 27, he was, braving the cold, saying his breviary walking round the garden he loved when a very small girl opened the gate, looked up at him— a bulky six feet of tough vitality—and said: "I am Bernadette Soubirous".

Bernadette, who had dealt calmly with police and magistrates, was undoubtedly nervous and, taken suddenly off his guard, the parish priest answered in a fashion less than fatherly: "So you're the little girl that they're telling these strange stories about!"

His tone, Bernadette recorded, was "not very agreeable". Nevertheless she started to give her message: "I have come from the Lady—".

"Yes, yes, I know. You claim to see visions and you're upsetting the whole countryside with your stories. Tell me about them."

At the conclusion of her account he asked: "Do you know this Lady's name?"

"No, M. l'Abbé, she doesn't tell me her name."

" Is she dumb?"

"If she had been dumb, M. l'Abbé, she could not have told me to come and see you."

"You know that those who believe your story are saying that the Lady is the Blessed Virgin herself?"

"I have not said so, M. l'Abbé."

"You understand that if you are lying in saying you have seen Our Lady in the grotto, you run the risk of never seeing her in reality in Heaven?"

"Yes, M. l'Abbé. All I know is that I see the Lady as clearly as I see you now and she talks to me as clearly as you are talking to me now and she said I was to come and tell you from her that she wants a chapel built on the rock at Massabielle."

"Then you will tell the Lady that the parish priest of

Lourdes is not in the habit of dealing with people he does not know. Let her say what her name is and prove that the name she gives is really hers."

(III)

The nature of the "proof" for which the parish priest asked is the now-famous request that she would make the wild-rose which hung in the grotto burst into flower. On the face of it, it was a simple demand for a miracle of nature —a rose suddenly blooming in February—and, as such, it has always been chronicled, almost as if it was the first thing that came into the Abbé Peyramale's head. But its significance surely lies very much deeper; and in asking for that specific "sign" he was already talking in Bernadette's own language. He was trying to explain to her, *in her own terms*, why he thought she was mistaken.

For the wild rose had a particular importance for her. Whether or not, in her narration to him, she had mentioned it, we have now no means of knowing (though his choice of it suggests that she had) but he was certainly quite well aware, from the reports of Father Pène and his sister, of what had happened during the week.

Two days earlier (according to the Pène account) when "the crowd touched the branches of the wild rose, Bernadette got up crying and went to clear the people away from them. We questioned her in our house, later in the day, asking her why she had done this? She answered: 'I was afraid that when they moved the branches they would make the Lady fall, because her feet were resting on the rose bush'. From that day on, the aunt who was with her used often to warn the crowd not to touch the rose bush".

In spite of the warning, the crowd did not always respect

that wish. On the next day—the day of the finding of the spring—when Bernadette had to move about, an independent (and sceptical) spectator, Mlle Lacrampe, the hotel owner, recorded: "She passed no more than a few yards from me. She moved the hanging branches of the rose bush carefully with one hand and went on without stopping . . . towards the back of the grotto. The crowd pressed close behind her and I could see by every movement of her body that she was upset, for she realized that the branches which she had moved with such care were being pushed about by the people. I noticed particularly sharp little backward movements of her head".

The wild briar was thus the one thing at the Grotto to which Bernadette attached very great importance, because the Lady's feet rested on it. If it were in very truth the Mother of God whose feet, each with a golden rose on it, touched the branches, was it not strange that the plant of the crown of thorns which she now made her footstool showed no signs of it? That, surely, is what the Abbé Peyramale meant and what Bernadette understood. The "sign" he asked for was for her as much as—if not more than—for himself.

"Ask the Lady", said the parish priest, "to make the wild briar blossom. If she has a right to a chapel, she will understand. If she does not understand, you can tell her she need not trouble to send any more messages to the parish priest of Lourdes."

That Our Lady did understand was to be amply demonstrated later, even though the wild-rose did not blossom.

(IV)

During the next two days, the Abbé Peyramale was subject to two opposing stresses. On the one hand, the crowds had increased to such an extent now that the spring had started to flow that police precautions were necessary to control them. The authorities called at the presbytery and informed the parish priest that they proposed issuing orders for a small detachment of infantry, gendarmes and municipal police to take the necessary safety measures. The Abbé expressed his gratitude, gave his approval and told them, to their satisfaction, of his interview with the bishop on Friday and Bernadette on Saturday. But on the Monday, the Abbé Dézirat, who was not under the Lourdes jurisdiction, visited the Grotto* and, completely convinced, gave his account of the matter to the Lourdes clergy. The Abbé Peyramale had thus, for the first time, detailed evidence from a priest and theologian. If it did not convince him, it must have at least unsettled him, and at Bernadette's next visit, his somewhat brutal over-emphasis masked the interior stress. It happened the following day, Tuesday, March 2.

When Bernadette returned from the Grotto that morning she told one of her aunts: "The Lady wants me to go to M. le Curé".

"O my God! Again?" said Basile Casterot, and at first refused to take her. But, in the end, she and her sister, Bernadette's godmother, went with her to beard the formidable parish priest once more. Aunt Basile, at least, was even more frightened of the Abbé than Bernadette was. "When I go anywhere near the reverend father", she admitted, "my knees begin to tremble and I get goose-flesh." And the reception was such that she never found the courage to go again.

"What have you come for this time?" asked the Abbé. "Has the wild briar blossomed or the Lady told you her name?"

* See p. 27.

"'The Lady wants you to have a procession to the Grotto'", said Bernadette.

"You little liar! How do you propose we should arrange it?" he stormed; and according to Aunt Basile, "prowled up and down the room in a rage" saying: "It is a wretched thing to have a family like this in the place. They turn it upside down and lead to nothing but disorder. We will do better than you ask. We will give you a torch all to yourself and you shall run your own procession. The people will follow you. *You* need no priests to arrange a procession".

"I don't say anything to anyone", said Bernadette. "I don't ask them to come with me."

Undoubtedly she was frightened. She "sat there all trussed up in her cape and never moved."

"I tell you you see nothing", said the Abbé. "A lady cannot come out of a hole! You haven't told me her name. It *can't* be anything. Why did you not ask her name?"

"I did", said Bernadette, "but she only laughed."

"You miserable child", thundered the parish priest. "To think of it! A Lady! A procession!" "It was terrible to see and hear him", recorded Aunt Basile, who did not, naturally, understand his dilemma, though it became obvious enough when he spoke to Bernadette again: "Be careful, child, you must be very sure of what you say. If your Lady exists and she is the Blessed Virgin—".

"I did not say that."

"No, she will not give her name. But if she is, we must carry out her wishes: but if she isn't and we have a procession, we shall do great harm to religion. You see that, don't you? What you have said is dreadfully serious. Are you absolutely certain she asked for a procession?"

For the first and last time, Bernadette hesitated. Then she said: "I think so".

"Then you are not sure," he shouted. "That is the

finishing touch. Either you are telling lies or else your Lady isn't what she pretends to be. And if she *does* want a procession, she should have sent you to the Bishop of Tarbes, not to me. Let me hear nothing of you again until she tells you her name and makes the wild rose blossom."

And, as he subsequently confided to friends, he made as though to seize the broom standing in the hall and lay it about the shoulders of the "little nuisance".

(v)

On the way home, Bernadette remembered that she had not told the Abbé that the Lady had also reiterated her request for a chapel. She wanted to return and give the message, but only wild horses would have dragged Aunt Basile, who was crying copiously, back to the presbytery. In fact, Bernadette was unable to persuade any of her family to accompany her there again and at last approached Dominiquette Cazenave, who had been among those at the Grotto for the past week and had come to believe in her.

Dominiquette accordingly went to the presbytery and informed the Abbé Peyramale: "The child who goes to the Grotto wants to see you again; her relations refuse to bring her; when may we come?"

"Bring her this evening at seven o'clock."

"M. le Curé, I do beg you not to frighten her."

"No, no. I won't."

"I'm only sorry you've not seen the girl in ecstasy," said Mlle Cazenave, as a parting shot. When she recounted the interview, she gave it as her opinion: "I think the parish priest believed in her but would not admit it".

During the day, the Abbé Peyramale had certainly thought of very little else. Not long after Bernadette had left, Father Pène had arrived and asked if there was any news.

"Yes, there is," said the Abbé, in a tone of triumph.

"What is it?"

"Then he told me," records Father Pène, "that Bernadette had faltered over the matter of the procession. When
he had finished he said in a sharp tone which was, all the
same, full of curiosity: 'Well, do you still believe in her?' "

"Why not?" said Father Pène.

" 'Oh, this is too much,' shouted the Abbé, with an
agitated movement of his head and hands. 'This is sheer
wishful thinking'."

Father Pène suggested alternatives: "This contradiction
of Bernadette's cannot lessen the force of what has already
happened," he said. "The child may have failed in her
mission on this one point. Some pious person may have put
this idea into her head. It may even be that the Devil has
put a spoke in the wheel and has thrown in this little black
spot to confuse us. Let us have patience till the drama is
over."

What had, in fact, happened was none of these things.
The Lady had said: "I want people to come here in procession". That, and nothing more. It was Bernadette (and
also, in fact, the Abbé Peyramale) who had interpreted this
as an immediate, instead of a general, request. Thus when
faced with the "dreadfully serious" question whether the
Lady really had asked the Abbé Peyramale to organize a
procession there and then, she was naturally "not sure".

The Abbé was at least determined to turn the evening
interview into a thorough cross-examination of the *voyante*
and settle the matter finally one way or the other. The whole
staff was there—Father Pène who believed in her; Father
Pomian, her confessor, who was wavering; and Father
Serre who remained polite but immovably sceptical.

Bernadette explained that she had returned because she

had forgotten to mention that the Lady had repeated her request for the chapel.

"The chapel!" said the Abbé Peyramale. "Is this like the procession—or are you sure?"

"About this, M. l'Abbé, I am quite certain."

"Then, as I said, you must ask her to tell you her name and to make the wild rose flower. When we know who she is, we will build her a very big chapel."

With this, he dismissed the matter and passed on to the cross-examination by the curates. This led nowhere, because of their difficulty of understanding the *patois*. One instance will suffice. When Father Pène asked her: "Tell us the words that the Lady in white said to you," he used the word "paraoulos" which, in the *patois* of his own neighbouring valley meant "words". But in the *patois* of the Lourdes valley it meant "crockery pots" and Bernadette, doing her best but frankly puzzled, explained: "There are no crockery pots at all down there".

(vi)

The last day of the "Great Fortnight", Thursday, March 4, was market day in Lourdes. There were at least ten thousand people at Massabielle (the police sergeant put it as high as 20,000) hoping for some spectacular miracle. It is probable that the Abbé Peyramale's request for the flowering of the wild briar was, by this time, generally known. Nothing out of the ordinary happened. It was obvious that Bernadette was talking to the Lady, as she had done on previous days; but there was no miracle—unless one shared Jacomet's opinion that the lack of accident in so dense a crowd, containing every trouble-making element, was a miracle in itself.

In the evening, Bernadette had her fourth interview with the parish priest. She was now no longer afraid of him and he, on his part, was becoming accustomed to her.

"I asked the Lady her name again, M. l'Abbé, but still she only smiled."

"Then I can do nothing. You understand that? If I knew it was the Blessed Virgin, I would do everything she asks; but, once again, as I do not know, I can do nothing. Did she tell you to return to the Grotto?

"No, M. l'Abbé."

"Then has she said she won't come back any more?"

"She has not said so."

"Well, if she does come back, beg her to tell you her name."

Even his kindness heightened the anti-climax. For the first time, Bernadette burst into tears. She did not visit the Grotto for three weeks.

(VII)

During those three weeks, the Abbé Peyramale became gradually reassured. Bernadette was behaving with outstanding normality. An observer at that time noticed: "She is a very level-headed girl, very candid, very pious and, above all, very gay. She attends the school conducted by the Sisters of Nevers, whose only complaint about her is her great ignorance. Her confessor gives her an excellent character. She has not been near the Grotto since March 4. She is very well and appears absolutely indifferent both to the admiration and the contempt with which she is treated".

The authorities, however, were of the opinion that she would be better out of the way and on Thursday, March 25—the Feast of the Annunciation—Lacadé, urged on by

Jacomet, wrote to the Prefect to ask if he should send her
to a mental home. The Prefect thought it advisable and
ordered a medical examination.

That morning Bernadette once more called at the
presbytery. She had once more felt the compulsion to go to
the Grotto and had there held a colloquy with Our Lady.

"What do you want today?" asked the parish priest.

Bernadette, without even saying Good-morning, said, in
patois: *"Qué soy l'Immaculado Counceptiou. Qué soy l'Immaculado Counceptiou!"*

Hearing this, the Abbé almost had an attack of vertigo.
As he admitted later in the morning, to M. Ribettes of the
grocery store: "The Lady said to Bernadette: 'I am the
Immaculate Conception'. I was so amazed by it that I felt
myself stagger and was on the point of falling". But all he
said to Bernadette was: "What's that you're saying, you
conceited little thing?"

" *'Qué soy l'Immaculado Counceptiou!'* It's the Lady who has
just said this to me."

"You are deceiving me. What does it mean, 'Immaculate
Conception'?"

"I don't know, M. l'Abbé."

"How can you say things you don't understand?"

"That's why I've been repeating it all the way from the
Grotto. So that I should get it right."

"I see. Well, I'll consider what is to be done."

And with this, he dismissed her.

The Lady had told her name. "The theologian in him,"
comments Mgr Trochu, "jumped when he grazed the
supernatural ... What if she were speaking the truth
today? What if the words had been uttered at Massabielle?
People tell lies with words they know, not with words they
do not understand! That these words 'Immaculate
Conception' were no more than sounds in Bernadette's

ears, M. Peyramale was to have as many proofs as he could desire."

His first care was to consult the mystical writers on the subject of diabolic possession. This might be a work of Satan, after all. But, in his heart, he seems to have been convinced. The best evidence for this is the gradual drawing away from him of the secular authorities who had valued him so highly when he was firm in his scepticism.

Dutour wrote to the Prefect, still praising him, of course, as "so intelligent, so zealous, so benevolent, so prudent", but adding: "Misled no doubt by some information which he has not checked with sufficient care, he has let it be seen that he is too much impressed by facts to which he would have denied all credence had he put less trust in the discernment and character of the persons who reported them to him".

Nevertheless the parish priest did not, as was generally expected, make a pronouncement from the pulpit on Easter Day, for now the utmost testing by time was essential. But he did, in no uncertain terms, prevent the attempt to incarcerate Bernadette in an asylum.

Three obliging doctors had provided the analysis that Bernadette had "psychological disturbances, the effects of which explain the phenomena of the vision", and Lacadé and Dutour had come to the "so intelligent, so zealous, so benevolent, so prudent" parish priest to ask his concurrence in their plan of confining her.

"Gentlemen," roared the Abbé, "Bernadette is delicate; she is poor: but you had better understand that she is not alone. The man who is responsible for her soul is here. On the spot. Kindly tell the Prefect that his gendarmes will have to pass over my dead body before they touch a hair of this child's head."

But though the Abbé was won over, he resisted his own

personal beliefs and announced: "I am waiting for episcopal authority to decide before making any announcement myself". It was nearly four years before the official decision was given, but Our Lady allowed the Abbé Peyramale his own "sign" long before then.

On the Feast of the Immaculate Conception—8 December 1858—he had permitted the Litany of Our Lady to be said in front of the Grotto. Almost immediately, a worrying obsession took hold of him. He was certain that Bernadette was not the victim of hallucinations, but once more he was haunted by the idea that she might be "Satan's puppet", like so many of the other hysterics and charlatans now in Lourdes. In humble prayer, he begged a personal favour of Our Lady. It was granted one Sunday at Mass.

"I noticed at the altar rails," he recorded, "someone with a bright halo round her head. I gave her Holy Communion without realizing who it was; but I followed her with my eyes until she was back in her place and when she turned round to kneel down, I recognized Bernadette Soubirous. From that moment, my anxieties ceased and I no longer had any doubt about the Apparitions."

Henceforth, his place in her life was to protect her and to prepare her, as far as he could, for her vocation of sanctity; to guard, above all, her humility. One story is so characteristic that it may do duty for all the rest. An American bishop came to see Bernadette and instinctively went down on his knees to kiss her hand. The Abbé Peyramale lifted him up rapidly and roughly and, pushing Bernadette down at his feet, said: "My Lord, bless this child".

So the parish priest started the training which was to be carried to its conclusion by the novice mistress.

VI

Bernadette and the Novice Mistress

As her name in religion, Bernadette took her actual baptismal name, Marie-Bernard. This was decided, independently of her, by the novice mistress, Mother Marie-Thérèse Vauzou, who explained: "It is only right that I should give her the name of the Blessed Virgin whose privileged child she is: at the same time I wanted to keep her patron's name, of which Bernadette is a diminutive".

For the understanding of Bernadette's years as a nun, a knowledge of the dominating novice mistress is important. It was she who was the instrument of the last and perhaps the greatest test of Bernadette's courage, the "martyrdom of the heart". In popular terms, Mother Vauzou has been made almost the "villain of the piece". To the end of her life, it is said, she did not believe Bernadette's claims and once, when the possibility of her canonization was spoken of, she exclaimed: "Let them wait till I am dead"—which was interpreted as meaning that she would have turned Devil's Advocate.

(1)

Mother Vauzou was forty-one when the twenty-two-year-old Bernadette came to Nevers. She had become a postulant at Saint-Gildard in the year Bernadette was born and now, in 1866, had been mistress of novices for five

years. Altogether she was to spend twenty years in that post
followed by eighteen more as Superior General before she
resigned her office to place herself at the orders of one of
her former novices and become a simple Sister of the or-
phanage at Lourdes. She was over eighty when she died in
1907, having "a prestige in the Community which was
unparalleled". Towards the end of her life it was said that
she was sometimes so affected by the demonstrations of the
crowds at the Grotto, which she could see from the window
of her room, that she would abruptly close the shutters. She
was heard to remark thoughtfully: "After all, the wild rose
did not blossom!"

But—we may be allowed to believe—immediately after
death she was active on Bernadette's behalf. The story of it,
though it belongs to the end, must be told at the beginning.
On the day after her death, in the presence of her body, the
Superior General, Mother Forestier, prayed to her: "Mother,
things do not always look the same in Heaven as they do on
earth. Now that you are, I trust, illuminated by the pure
light above, be so good as to take Bernadette's cause in
hand. I leave the initiative in this matter to you. I shall not
take any steps myself. I shall wait for a sign from Heaven".
A fortnight later, the Superior General received a letter
from Rome, which she believed to be the sign. It asked her
without delay to collect evidence from all who had known
Bernadette for use in a possible canonization cause.

Marie-Thérèse Vauzou's father and grandfather were
both lawyers. She belonged, that is to say, to the upper
provincial middle-class which, in nineteenth-century France,
attached an altogether disproportionate importance to birth
and breeding. Nor, it seems, did she ever quite conquer a
certain snobbery, as her almost incredible remark to her
secretary bears witness: "Oh, Bernadette was only a little
peasant girl. I cannot understand why the Blessed Virgin

appeared to her. There are so many others so refined and
well-bred".

To the limitations of this social background was added
the handicap of a naturally imperious temperament. "Her
intelligence and determination gave her even before her
First Communion a certain dominance over her companions", it is recorded, "and even at that age she liked to try
them out to see if she could be sure of their submission." As
novice mistress, she imposed "penances" which consisted
of kneeling down and kissing repeatedly the tiled floor.
She insisted that no novice should have any secrets from
her, and punishèd them by a searing "frigidity" if she
thought they had. Her key-words were "to belabour a
soul", "to use the shears", "to pulverize hearts". She had,
according to one of her secretaries, "a passion for shaping
souls. She could find the right chisel for each, and wield it".

"Now that we have you," she said to Bernadette on her
arrival, "we can knock you into shape."

"I hope you will do it gently," said Bernadette.

Mother Vauzou accepted the challenge.

For it was nothing less than a challenge, and the long,
intense struggle that followed for the prize of salvation was
something different from what may be called that routine
inculcation of humility to which Cardinal Verdier referred
when he remarked: "Humble Bernadette, hidden behind the
convent walls, in the midst of her trials of every kind,
appeared to have to apologise for the favours she had
received".

One of Bernadette's biographers, Mgr Trochu, has seen
in the relationship between her and Mother Vauzou
"simply a mutual lack of understanding between two
greatly gifted but entirely incompatible natures". Another,
Fr Henri Petitot, O.P., writing as a religious, explains:
"One need not be very intimately acquainted with the

religious life to realize that, only too often, beneath the most supernatural motives, are hidden likes or dislikes which are not supernatural but are inspired by temperament, by certain affinities, and by instinctive and even quite unsuspected natural aversions". And, at the canonization proceedings, Mother Bordenave declared: Mother "Marie-Thérèse Vauzou satisfied her strict and sensitive conscience that the excessive severity with which she had treated Sister Marie-Bernard was inspired by the necessity of humiliating her because of her wonderful mission, but it is certain she did not like Bernadette. When she spoke to me of the Venerable Bernadette, she never betrayed any feeling of affection for her. The mistress of novices herself did not realize the influences to which she was subjected".

In all these judgments there is an element of truth and yet, the more one tries to understand Mother Vauzou, the more inadequate they seem. And, to put them in perspective, it must be remembered that Bernadette declared with complete sincerity: "I owe her much gratitude for the good she did to my soul" and that Mother Vauzou, "tormented" as she said "by the fear that I was too hard on her", went to a Cistercian priest renowned for his sanctity to put the case before him and to make her confession. On leaving she said to her companion: "My mind is quite at ease now; I told the reasons for my behaviour and Fr Jean completely reassured me".

(II)

In trying to form a picture of Mother Marie-Thérèse Vauzou, her name in religion is not irrelevant, for she has about her something of the great Teresa of Avila. Her photograph shows a face more masculine than feminine,

with a high forehead, a commanding nose, a powerful chin
and eyes at once authoritative and sensitive. She had in
abundant measure, as we know, the Teresian gift of
organization and command. She could and did inspire, like
Teresa, an overwhelming affection and loyalty in her
novices and her nuns. Occasionally her recorded sentences
have a Teresian ring: "Out in the world they long for
prosperity and happiness; but for you all I wish two things:
humiliation and mortification". To one who said: "I ask
God to let me love Him as you love Him", she answered,
with a deep sigh: "You are not asking very much". On the
other hand she had nothing of Teresa's mysticism. She was
a woman "more of action than of contemplation". And she
was not a saint. Moreover, precisely those attributes of her
patron which she lacked Bernadette possessed. It was
Bernadette who shared Teresa's mystical certainty as, on
another plane, she had her simplicity of perception, her
devastating "common sense".

It must be remembered, too, that under the stern appearance was a disposition "lively, intense, impulsive". The
crushing discipline she administered to others Mother
Vauzou had first applied to herself. "Beneath her cold
exterior," says Mother Forestier, "there was a strong desire
to give and receive much affection". And, at the beginning,
such affection was given to and received from Bernadette.

There is the revealing story of the occasion when Mother
Vauzou returned to the House after a few days' absence, to
find her novices waiting to welcome her and being greeted
by Bernadette who ran forward and flung herself into her
arms "like a child deprived for a long time of its mother".
When someone said later to Bernadette: "What excitement
at meeting your mistress again!" she replied: "Yes; it was
much too natural of me, wasn't it? I repented of it very
greatly".

On another occasion, Bernadette was sitting on the step of her desk sewing while Mother Vauzou was explaining the catechism to the novices. After the lesson, the mistress called one of the novices to her and asked: "Why were you looking like that at Sister Marie-Bernard?"

"I was thinking," said the novice, "that you must have been very happy to have Bernadette so close to you."

"I should have been just as happy," Mother Vauzou replied, "to have had any one of you beside me. Bernadette is on the common road."

Towards the end of Bernadette's life, she was once walking very painfully because of her tumour on the knee when she met in the cloister Mother Vauzou who made some remark to her which wrung from her a wounded: "Oh, Mother!" The nuns who heard it were scandalized that she should so answer and Mother Vauzou commented: "Ah! We have wounded your little self-esteem!"

It should be unnecessary to insist that in the two latter cases the remarks were made in particular and difficult situations in public and can hardly be taken at their face value as a deliberate wounding of Bernadette. Nor can they be adequately assessed without reference to the implications of the first.

In considering any characters there is always the danger that, almost unconsciously, we localize them, statically, "caught" in a particular "moment", like Pirandello's *Six Characters in search of an Author*. Bernadette tends to be, in our thought, a small girl of fourteen, because that is how we first meet her. And Mother Vauzou appears as an elderly, disciplined woman. But at the time of the 'Oh, Mother!' incident, Bernadette was thirty-three and Mother Vauzou fifty-one. The eighteen-and-a-half-year gap between them was at its seeming-narrowest. They were, theoretically, of equal status, for Mother Vauzou, still novice mistress, had

not yet become Superior General. And spiritually, Bernadette was the stronger of the two. Whatever is in question
here, it has no relation to a hard old woman wounding a
sick child.

The key to the relationship surely lies in the danger to
Bernadette of "a too particular attachment". This tempta-
tion the "impulsive, affectionate" Mother Vauzou had
known and conquered in herself before she saw and
recognized the possibility of it in Bernadette. "St Marie-
Bernard's great danger," writes Fr Petitot, "when she
donned the veil of the Sisters of Nevers was not so much
that she might be tempted to vanity or vain-glory, but that
she might be unwittingly carried away, with the most
genuinely good intentions, by passionate and absorbing
affection. This danger was doubly great because of her cold,
reserved manner, since it did not deceive her intimate
companions who were fully aware of her great capacity for
loving . . . When Bernadette entered the Nevers novitiate,
the older and more observant nuns may have foreseen that
she would be greatly attached to the mistress of novices."

When one adds to this the universal testimony of the
nuns that Mother Vauzou was of an almost identical nature
and that—as Mother Bordenave put it at the canonization
proceedings—"one was drawn to her as to a lover"; and
when it is remembered that, in the beginning, no one who
saw it doubted the great affection which existed between
the two, the nature of Mother Vauzou's training of her
privileged charge becomes clearer.

It is also clear that Bernadette herself understood and
co-operated with it. When she was asked whether Mother
Vauzou's hardness made her unhappy, she answered
immediately: "Oh no, she is quite right to behave in that
way". Once when the assistant infirmarian secured the
services of one of Bernadette's friends from Lourdes, she

was not allowed to continue indefinitely in the office and Bernadette, missing her, asked if she were ill. The answer was: "No, but Mother Mistress has forbidden me to have her again".

"I understand," said Bernadette.

On another occasion, a nun who was very fond of Bernadette and who said, "I am happy as long as I am near her," passed many nights at her bedside. Bernadette, in spite of her affection for her, always sent her away with "It makes me unhappy to see you there; go away, to please me". Nevertheless, the nun kept returning. An observer of this scene said to her: "I do not think God will leave you here very long; you are too fond of Bernadette", and soon afterwards the presentiment came true.

During a retreat, one of the nuns, Sister Campy, records: "I was waiting my turn outside the door of Mother Vauzou's room when the bell for conference rang. This meant I should have to leave and, seeing I should miss my turn, I showed signs of impatience, for I had been waiting for two days. Sister Marie-Bernard, who was on her way to instructions, tapped me on the shoulder, saying: 'Here is someone who is getting impatient'. I turned to her and said: 'But I have been waiting for two days!' She answered, with a little shrug: 'Ah! that doesn't matter!' "

(III)

By the end, at whatever cost to Bernadette's heart—and her own—Mother Vauzou had done the duty which had been entrusted to her and the nature of which she alone perhaps saw in its fullness. Her private "report", as novice mistress, on Bernadette was "*Caractère raide, très susceptible; modeste, pieuse, dévouée, elle a de l'ordre*". The second part—

"unassuming, pious, devoted, orderly"—suggests that she was as aware as anyone else that the "little self-esteem" of Bernadette—which, in public, she was supposed to be deflating—did not in fact exist. The first part—"rigid character, very susceptible"—is an exact description of the outer control masking the inward affection which was Bernadette's temperament.

But both *susceptible* and *raide* are words with various *nuances* of meaning, and when, years later, Mother Bordenave made the notes public, she felt it her duty to comment on this judgment. On *raide*, which she construed as "stubborn", she wrote: "This is rather one of the characteristics of the Pyrenean temperament, especially of the people from the Upper Pyrenees". For *susceptible*, which she took in the sense of "touchy", she suggested the substitution of *sensible*—which conveys a fragile sensitivity rather than a strong impulsiveness.

Though the legend has adopted Mother Bordenave's gloss, the facts support Mother Vauzou's exactitude.

In the world, standing like a rock against surrounding scepticism, the *caractère raide* had, humanly speaking, been Bernadette's salvation. In the convent, the "undue susceptibility" had to be overcome for the character to become complete in its heroic, lonely integrity; and it can hardly be a coincidence that the instrument of that "martyrdom of the heart" was a woman who had, because she shared it, an unrivalled knowledge of the temperament with which she was dealing and who "wielded the chisel" not, indeed, gently, but unerringly and with love. Without her, one is tempted to think, Bernadette might have found more difficulty in attaining that completion of surrender which was her final sanctity, and which was manifested when, shortly before she died, "she asked that all the pictures which had been previously hung on her bed to satisfy her devotion should be taken away. When asked the reason, she pointed to the crucifix and said: 'That is enough for me'."

Mgr Trochu quotes "some simple but profound words written at a time when justice on a magnificent scale was beginning to be rendered to Bernadette"—"To become a Saint our little Sister had only to let herself be fashioned first of all by the Blessed Virgin and then by her mistress of novices, and finally to humble herself." This judgment may be set beside that of Mother Bordenave at the canonization process: "I can affirm that had Mother Marie-Thérèse been able to penetrate this soul, she would have been so delighted with it that her affection for her novice might perhaps have been excessive and the holiness of Sister Marie-Bernard would have lost thereby". (One need only ask whether, considering her character and the circumstances, the novice mistress is likely to have allowed any person but herself to know the extent of her knowledge of and love for Bernadette.)

Moreover, there is some reason to suppose that Mother Vauzou was quite consciously what may be described as a co-operator with Our Lady in thus preparing Bernadette for sanctity. The dangers she instinctively recognized on the natural plane seemed to be confirmed by Our Lady herself, for Bernadette made no secret that she had been told not to allow herself to grow too fond of one of her cousins and, as Fr Petitot has pointed out, "it was undoubtedly Our Lady of Lourdes who warned her". Our Lady, too, had told Bernadette that she would not be happy in this life. In fact, her chief cause of unhappiness was the chilling distance which, after their first affectionate intimacy, Mother Vauzou enforced between them. Had Bernadette been allowed to give free reign to her great and reciprocated love for her "dear mistress", happiness might have hidden the way to Calvary.

G

The conventional explanation of the "rift", which
Bernadette's biographers assume, is surely sadly wide of the
mark. "The mistress of novices", says Fr Petitot, "was
imperious and had that domineering nature which exacts
complete submission even from those it loves, which
instinctively longs for absolute possession and if it meets
with any obstacle breaks it down, but love then changes to
hatred . . . If, with the permission of the Blessed Virgin,
Bernadette had revealed those secrets (concerning her
interior life) to Mother Marie-Thérèse for herself alone, the
mistress of novices would quickly have cherished and
protected her." And Mgr Trochu writes: "Mother Vauzou
felt herself checked on the threshold of this soul. Hence two
unfortunate results: she did not understand her and this both
hurt and vexed her. Imagining the check to her zeal was
entirely the novice's fault, she branded as indifference and
coarse obtuseness what was in the other mere reserve and
possibly supernatural prudence. Would not Sister Marie-
Bernard have misgivings on one particular point? The
Virgin of the grotto had sealed her lips on three secrets, on
a mysterious prayer for herself alone, and on other matters
possibly entirely personal, perhaps certain directions from
Our Lady concerning her future. Suppose that by allowing
a mistress of such dominating authority to penetrate the
recesses of her soul, she were to find herself induced to
reveal to her what she had no right to reveal to any
creature . . . ?"

The implication here is that Mother Vauzou was, in
every way, false to her mission—in the first place by giving
and encouraging an extravagant personal affection which
might have led Bernadette to betray Our Lady's secrets and,
in the second, when Bernadette refused the confidences, of
behaving with a calculated cruelty born of wounded pride.
This analysis might, indeed, be fitting for characters and

situations in Proust's world; but it has less than no relevance
to the real people at Saint-Gildard where the quest for
sanctity was being undertaken by two women who loved
God, Our Lady and each other.

(IV)

Bernadette's own spontaneous and unwavering defence
of Mother Vauzou's attitude from first to last is worth more
than all the testimony of spectators who, merely because
they were on the outside, judged what they saw by the
yardstick of their own experience and prejudices. Sister
Pascal, for example, records that on the occasion of some
festivity, "lots were drawn for a little statue of St Germaine
Cousin and it was won by Sister Marie-Bernard. There upon
Mother Marie-Thérèse Vauzou remarked in an ironical
tone: 'A shepherd girl could only fall into the hands of a
shepherd girl'." To see this as an example of Mother
Vauzou's snobbery and coldness tells us something about
Sister Pascal, but not necessarily anything about Mother
Vauzou and Bernadette. It is worth examining more
closely.

St Germaine Cousin was born in 1579 and died in 1601.
From her birth she seemed destined to suffer. Her father
ignored her, her step-mother ill-treated her. She was used as
the shepherdess of the poor family flock, sleeping in a
stable or in the garret. Poor as she was, she gave away all
she could to those even poorer. She had a great devotion to
Our Lady and to the Blessed Sacrament. It seems that Our
Lady wrought a miracle in her favour by making it possible
for her to cross a swollen river on her way to Mass. The
villagers, who had till then been inclined to deride her,
began to treat her as an object of veneration. One summer

morning, at a point when all were beginning to realize the
beauty of her life, her father, finding that she had not risen
at her usual time, went to call her and found her dead on her
pallet of vine-twigs. She was twenty-two. When, forty-three
years later, the grave was opened to receive another of the
family, her body was found to be fresh and perfectly preserv-
ed. A series of extraordinary cures were thereafter wrought
at her relics, freshly interred in a leaden coffin, until, during
the French Revolution, four atheists desecrated the grave and
threw quicklime and water on the body. After the Revolution the body was found to be still intact except where the
quicklime had done its work. In 1854—the year of the
dogmatic definition of the Immaculate Conception—she
was beatified and on the feast of SS. Peter and Paul, 1867,
almost on the first anniversary of Bernadette's coming to
Nevers, she was canonized. In her statues she is represented
with a sheep-dog or a sheep.

It would have been difficult to find any saint in the entire
calendar who was more appropriate, by every circumstance,
to Bernadette. Germaine had died at the age that Bernadette
now was, after having achieved, by loneliness, mortification
and the withdrawing of human affection, the goal to which
Bernadette was now travelling by the same road. Her
special devotion to Our Lady and the Blessed Sacrament
were the same as Bernadette's.

There was another, human circumstance. Bernadette
was not a shepherd-girl, though for that short time at
Bartrès she had looked after the sheep with no companion
but the favourite dog, "Pigou", and had found in the sun
and the solitude a relief from the overcrowded *cachot*. Those
days, during the summer months when she was, for the
first time, attending the catechism class, were some of the
happiest in her childhood. And this, certainly, Mother
Vauzou must have known. And when she said—was it

"ironically", as it sounded to Sister Pascal, or merely detachedly?—"A shepherd girl could only fall into the hands of a shepherd girl" (and, again, did she really say "a" or was it "the"?) she was surely speaking to her with a wealth of intimate meaning which only Bernadette fully understood.

It is probable that were we able to know fully the true circumstances of all the "episodes" recorded by those who saw but did not altogether understand, we should judge them differently. Even that cry of "Oh, Mother!", as Bernadette passed in the cloister, may have meant: "There is no need for this any longer", for Mother Vauzou's reply: "So we have wounded your little self-esteem!" was so obviously a "public" utterance which had no relevance to the true condition of Bernadette. And against all the public "snubs" must be set other scenes, too often forgotten because they do not fit in to the conventional picture.

Bernadette, when she was professed, was given a privilege which may have been unique and was certainly "almost unheard of at Saint-Gildard". She was permitted to visit the novitiate and to take her recreation with the novices. She was allowed, that is to say, free and continuous access to Mother Vauzou. Though the permission came from the Superior General, Mother Josephine Imbert, there can be little doubt (all chroniclers are unanimous in stressing the Superior General's deference to and even dependence on the novice mistress) that this arrangement was due to Mother Vauzou.

Moreover, Mother Vauzou gave her a post of some distinction. It was Bernadette who recited the public Rosary in the noviceship and "blessed the Hour". On at least one occasion she was commissioned to answer a letter from a lady of high rank in Mother Vauzou's name; at least one postulant was committed to her care. On another occasion, when Mother Vauzou was unable to deal with a postulant who was in tears and would not be comforted, she sent for Bernadette and said: "Sister, here is a poor child who has just come and is already 'in the dumps', poor little thing! Embrace her, Sister Marie-Bernard".

The often-told story of Bernadette entering the hall of the novitiate and being ordered sharply by Mother Vauzou to kiss the ground and withdraw needs the full setting and its sequel for true evaluation.

It occurred in the days when Bernadette was no longer a novice. Mother Vauzou was reading to the novices Lasserre's just-published book on "The Marvels of Lourdes". She did not hear Bernadette come in through the door at the back of the hall, but as soon as she saw her she said: "Sister Marie-Bernard, this is not the time to come in here. Kiss the ground and withdraw." Bernadette immediately obeyed, but before she reached the door again, Mother Vauzou said: "Sister Marie-Bernard, come here". Bernadette went and knelt by her chair and told her the reason for her coming, which concerned an invalid Sister about whom she wanted immediate advice. After she had given her decision, Mother Vauzou "laid her hand on Bernadette's head—which with her was a gesture of love and protection. Then she added: 'You may go, daughter'."

In 1875 (that is to say, two years before the "Oh, Mother" episode), Mother Vauzou seems to have been satisfied that Bernadette's mastery of herself was now such that there was no danger of "self-esteem" of any kind—if, indeed, she had ever really supposed that there was—and during an evening reunion she "sent for Sister Marie-Bernard to come and sit beside the Mothers, nearer the statue of the Blessed Virgin".

Other examples could be given, but enough has been said to suggest the real nature of Mother Vauzou's training of Bernadette. In an unrivalled way, she, more than any other human being, helped Bernadette to fulfil her aspiration:

"O Jesus and Mary, grant that my only consolation in this world may be to love you and suffer for sinners. O my Jesus, grant me the holy jealousy of divine love, redeem, attract and elevate all my affections".

(v)

Were this a study of Mother Vauzou, one might be tempted to probe into the problem of how far her heart, too, was martyred and how greatly she, lacking Bernadette's resources, suffered; but, here, all that is relevant is her alleged disbelief in Bernadette and her supposed blindness to her quality.

The charges may, surely, be dismissed at once. If no one heard her, in conversation, express affection for Bernadette, that was to be expected. It would have been more surprising if she had. If she insisted that Bernadette was a "good ordinary nun" and "on the common road", she was doing no more than her duty to all the other novices in her charge whom, no less than Bernadette, she had to shape for salvation and who might have wondered, with the famous "confidante of Our Lady" in their midst, whether they were not, in comparison, handicapped. In emphasizing the "ordinariness" Mother Vauzou was only confirming Bernadette's own vehement protest to a questioner:

"Our Lady promised to make you happy in the next world?"

"Yes."

"So you are sure of going to Heaven?"

"No, no, no!"

"What! Not after the Blessed Virgin's promise?"

"Oh, but that makes no difference. Only if I am good."

"But didn't she tell you what to do to go to Heaven?"

"No, Monsieur: we knew that quite well before."

If Mother Vauzou recalled that the rose-bush did not blossom, it may have been a reminder that one should not ask for "signs", not a suggestion that it ought to have done. That the remark at least implied no disbelief in the Apparitions is obvious from her other dictum that "Our Lady showed her excellent taste by choosing so beautiful a place as Lourdes". And the last words of Mother Vauzou, whose life-long devotion had been to Our Lady of Sorrows, were: "Our Lady of Lourdes, protect me in the hour of my death . . ."

VII

Bernadette and Our Lady

"DID you see the Lady?" one of the visitors to the Grotto was asked.
"No, but I saw Bernadette."

The most important part of the story can never be written, because it concerns the relation of Bernadette to Our Lady; but here and there, breaking through to the surface of events which is called history, certain indications have reached us.

One obstacle to such understanding as we might have is the statue of Our Lady of Lourdes.

Bernadette's insistence on Our Lady's beauty, reiterated again and again, is almost hyperbolic: "So beautiful that when one has seen her, it is impossible to love anything else on earth" . . . "so beautiful that one only thinks of dying in order to see her again" . . . She was shown an album of pictures of the Blessed Virgin by great artists. Opening it at the Renaissance masterpieces, she shut the book with a cry of horror—a tribute to her immediate perception of the diabolic quality of the epoch. She was told there were others and shown a painting by Fra Angelico whose one recorded saying was "to paint the things of Christ, the artist must live with Christ". Bernadette admitted they were better, but that they were not like Our Lady. At last she found one which, though not exactly a "likeness" at least had something in common with the

Mother of God and recalled her in some recognizable way—the old stylized Byzantine painting of the Madonna, traditionally attributed to St Luke.

When Fabisch, the sculptor, was at last commissioned to make, as far as possible to Bernadette's specifications, the marble statue which now stands in the Grotto, she did her best to explain to him, but he ignored even her elementary instructions, such as that "she was short rather than tall and appeared very young" and so far failed to capture any of the reality of the Vision that, when Bernadette was asked whether it was like the Blessed Virgin, she answered: "Not in the least".

On the day of its dedication, both she and the Abbé Peyramale were too ill to attend the ceremony, but when, later, she first saw the statue, she could not help running away immediately since, according to Dr Dozous, an eye-witness, she could not endure the sight of such an image as that. On the subsequent occasions when she prayed in the Grotto, she kept her eyes shut so that she might not see it.

Even allowing for Fabisch's lack of talent, one has to remember—to quote J. K. Huysmans—"that he had seen Bernadette in a state of ecstasy, and therefore had seen a human face illumined with a reflection of the divine, and all it resulted in was this effigy of a young first communicant, this vapid and slack personification of insipidity".

Today the statue is so well known throughout the world that, inevitably if subconsciously, it obtrudes itself between us and the reality of that unique relationship. It may be that we should understand Our Lady better by looking direct at Bernadette.

Though it would be impossible, of course, to call Bernadette a "mirror of Our Lady", it is surely true that certain qualities of Our Lady are mirrored in her; and that the Queen of Heaven's choice of this particular handmaid was of more than usual consequence we may guess from the fact of Bernadette's canonization. She was not a passive instrument of revelation, like the children of La Salette or Fatima or many others to whom Our Lady appeared. She was herself a saint.

And the more one meditates on the story, the more indications seem to reveal themselves. Is the fact that Our Lady showed herself as a child of sixteen—as she was at the time of the Annunciation when she became "the handmaid of the Lord"—altogether irrelevant? At that same age, in a border town of mixed nationalities, did not she, bearing her Secret, have to face the gossip, the suspicion, the hostility of a small community, as, centuries later, her own handmaid had to face it? Is there not, common to both, the same unquestioning obedience, the same humility, the same courage? The difference between "our tainted nature's solitary boast" and the nineteenth-century Pyrenean girl is, on one plane, overwhelming; but, because of Mary's complete humanity, it is a difference of degree not of kind; and there may be worse ways of directing our meditation on Our Lady's hidden years at Nazareth than to study Bernadette at Lourdes.

These are mysteries. The answers can never be given; but, in such a study as this, it is permissible to ask them because they are factors in the problem. The challenge of Bernadette involves in a special way the challenge of Our Lady. And though the appearance and the circumstance are quite different, one cannot help thinking that Bernadette, who turned from Fabisch's statue in horror, would have recognized, just as she did in the old Byzantine painting, something of Our Lady in Chesterton's description of her as King Alfred saw her when the heathen hosts were all but victorious:

One instant in a still light,
He saw Our Lady then,
Her dress was soft as western sky,
And she was a queen most womanly—
But she was a queen of men.
Over the iron forest
He saw Our Lady stand,
Her eyes were sad, withouten art,
And seven swords were in her heart—
But one was in her hand.

And if at Massabielle she held a rosary, was not that itself a sword, and was not the Feast of the Holy Rosary, for the most specific of historical reasons, the date of the battle of Lepanto?*

(II)

The relationship between Our Lady and Bernadette, as we are permitted to know it, contains two episodes which, considered together, may throw some light on it.

During the period of the Apparitions, a visiting Abbé was allowed to question Bernadette.

"Is it true that you have seen the Blessed Virgin?"

"Yes, M. l'Abbé."

"I don't believe you have seen her."

Bernadette made no answer and he persisted: "Well, won't you answer me?"

"What do you want me to say?"

"You should convince me that you have seen her."

"Oh, she didn't tell me to make anyone believe it."

* October 7th, 1571. At the battle of Lepanto, Don John of Austria defeated the enormous power of the Turks in Europe, which, but for this victory, would have meant the triumph of Islam over Christendom. From this point of view, it ranks with Charles Martel's victory at Tours. The battle was almost a forlorn hope and was won, so we may believe, because the Pope, from dawn till night, remained in his oratory, continuously saying the Rosary. The day was thereafter appointed the Feast of the Most Holy Rosary and so has remained.

"There are many other girls better than you and more worthy of the favours of Heaven."

"Of course."

"Then why should she choose you?"

"I suppose because that is how it seemed to her."

"You must be very proud."

"Why?"

"If I were in your place I should be very proud."

"Oh, she merely looks on me as a servant."

"You are a servant of the Blessed Virgin, then?"

"Yes."

"What wages does she pay you?"

"Oh," said Bernadette, smiling slightly, "we have not fixed that yet."

"But what do you think she will give you?"

Bernadette, who knew from experience that Lourdes employers insisted on a trial period before finally engaging their servants or agreeing on their wages, said: "She will dismiss me after the trial period".

The other story concerns her life in the convent. The Mother Superior suddenly fell ill at a time when she was overwhelmed with work. She sent for Bernadette and explained that "she hadn't time to be ill". Would Bernadette speak to Our Lady about it? She recovered immediately.

Finally, one may instance, as an example of the understanding to which the Bernadette "who could not meditate" attained, the acrostic she composed — it is in her notebook — on the names of Jesus and Mary in which "the virtues seem to hold a mysterious balance".

J oie	M ortification
E spérance	A mour
S ouffrance	R égularité
U nion	I nnocence
S oumission	A bandon

The spiritual implications are worth studying.

(III)

God, through Our Lady: Our Lady, through Bernadette, gave a hundred years ago at Lourdes an unmistakable "sign" in history. Our Lady's message, Bernadette's individuality, the miraculous cures, are so interwoven that, in the end, they cannot be considered except as a unity. Each contributes its own part to the understanding of the whole.

It is difficult to see how, in good faith, the challenge can be ignored and one is tempted to think that, if the world has not been converted, it is because the inevitable conclusion dare not be faced. On the intellectual level, it means—as M. Jean Guitton's analysis (which is quoted at the beginning of this essay) makes quite clear—an admission of the unique truth of the Roman Catholic Church as it is today.

The real challenge, however, lies much deeper and the meaning of it has been so well expressed by J. K. Huysmans that I make no apology for quoting him at length. The author of *A Rebours*, of all men, cannot be suspected of not "knowing life".

"These apparitions of the Virgin, attested as they are by such unheard of acts, are indeed very disquieting for many people, if you come to think of it. Take, for instance, the case of a man, not a rascal with a corrupted conscience, but an honest fellow who has not the faith or has lost it, just as many others have done, on leaving college, when the increasing power of the senses is making itself felt. If he remembers the teaching of the catechism, he regards it as childish and is almost astonished that he could ever have been naïve enough to believe it. Moreover, he observes that the few practising Catholics of his acquaintance are more stupid than the rest—and, what is worse, they are no better than himself—and then his position is settled: religion is all right for the weak-minded and for women and children; every man of education and sense must shake himself free of it . . . And now it is roughly and bluntly brought home to him, and by those upon whose good sense he can rely, that the Virgin is working miracles at Lourdes. Well then, she exists! And, if she exists, Christ is God and, as surely as thread follows needle, he has to acknowledge that the teaching of the catechism, which he thought so childish, is not so; then, the Church and all her dogmas are binding.

"And here the trouble begins. If he hearkens to his conscience, he has to give up a host of pleasures in this world and turn his life upside down at the feet of a priest. If he does not do so, owing to human respect and cowardice, he is in a permanent state of simmering uneasiness and self-reproach. And so our honest fellow prefers to blindfold himself and know nothing. It matters little to sceptics of this stamp whether the arguments against Lourdes be sound or futile; they have not the least desire to go into them. This explains why the clinic, though thrown so widely open to everyone, is so little frequented by unbelievers. It has against it what may be called the hatred of fear, of the fear of the Faith."

But the challenge is not to unbelievers only. Indeed, not primarily. Bernadette feared only one thing in this world— "bad Catholics". Three times reiterated, Our Lady's challenge rings down the years: "Penance! Penance! Penance!"

London
Our Lady, Mother of Divine Providence, 1957.